AF395048

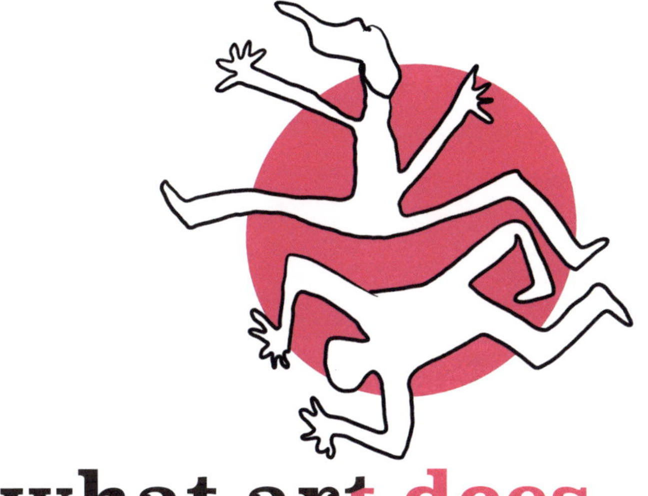

what art does

an unfinished theory

BRIAN ENO
BETTE A.

faber

First published in the UK and the USA in 2025
by Faber & Faber Ltd
The Bindery, 51 Hatton Garden
London EC1N 8HN

First published in a limited edition in the UK in 2024
by Opal Limited and Bette Adriaanse

Design by Nick Robertson
Printed in Slovenia

A CIP record for this book
is available from the British Library

ISBN 978–0–571–39551–4

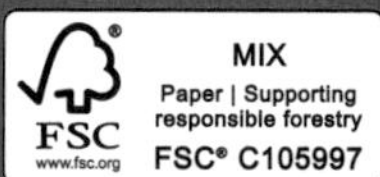

Printed and bound in the EU on FSC® certified paper in line with our continuing
commitment to ethical business practices, sustainability and the environment
For further information see faber.co.uk/environmental-policy

Our authorised representative in the EU for product safety is Easy Access
System Europe, Mustamäe tee 50, 10621 Tallinn, Estonia
gpsr.requests@easproject.com

6 8 10 9 7 5

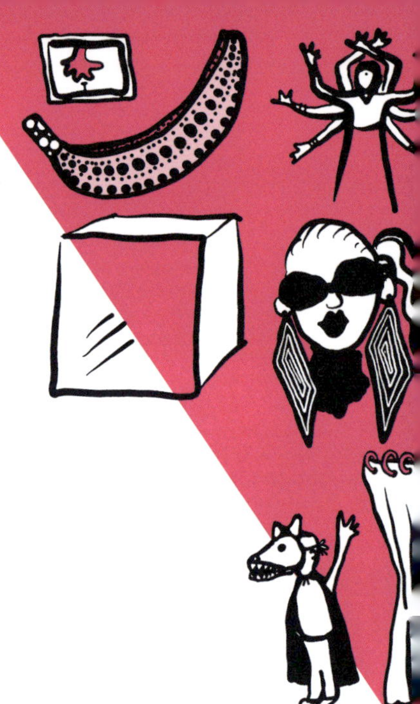

1 art

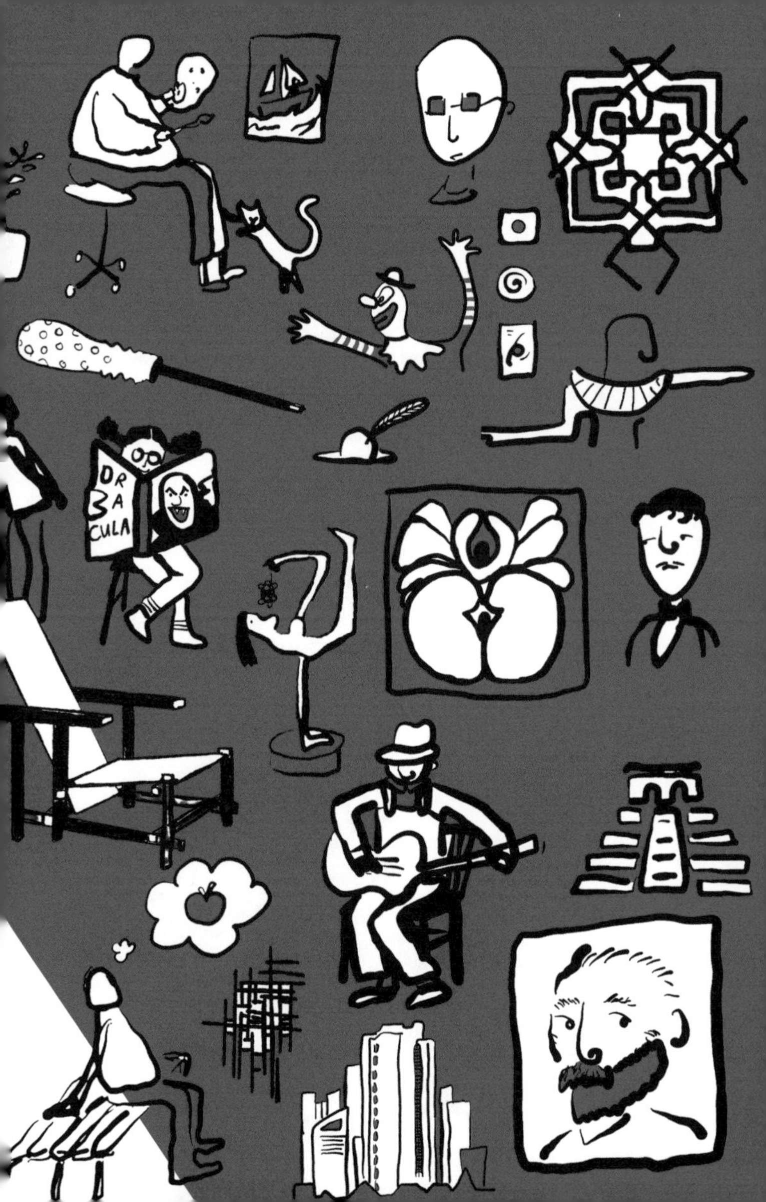

DR
3
A
CULA

making **art** seems to be a universal human activity

All over the world, people can be found creating and wearing elaborate costumes pretending to be something else: a dangerous animal, a king, someone from the spirit world.

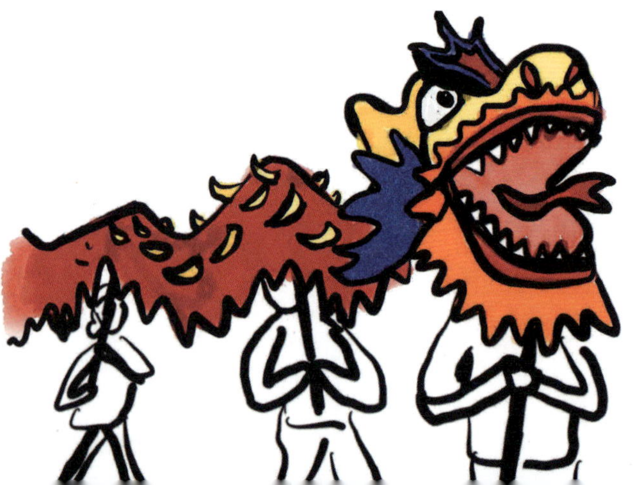

All over the world people decorate themselves and their surroundings with patterns, shapes and colours, and construct references to places, people and events that aren't now and here. We don't know of any human group that doesn't do art in some form or another, and usually in many different forms.

We could say that art is one of the key attributes of being human, like language. It's easy to understand why language is so universal, but we don't seem to have a very clear picture of why art should also be.

Why does every culture spend such a large part of its free time in 'made-up worlds' like books, plays, paintings, dances, movies, self-decoration, stories and songs – all the things we might call art? What are we doing there? Why did humanity develop them, and why do we value them?

It isn't enough to say: 'Well, they're nice and we enjoy them.' Why do we find them enjoyable? Isn't 'being enjoyable' nature's way of getting us to do something? Fruits are sweet and enjoyable because eating them is good for your health and growth (and good for the fruit whose seeds are thus spread). Sex is enjoyable because your genes just love perpetuating themselves and do so by producing more gene-machines like you.

We understand why science, for example, is important: it helps us understand how the material world works and puts us in a better position to enter into fruitful relationships with it.

This need not be the conscious motivation of an individual scientist, just as 'improving my health' isn't necessarily why we eat strawberries; but nonetheless that is the result. We can easily explain the existence of science by the benefits it produces for us.

But what does art do?

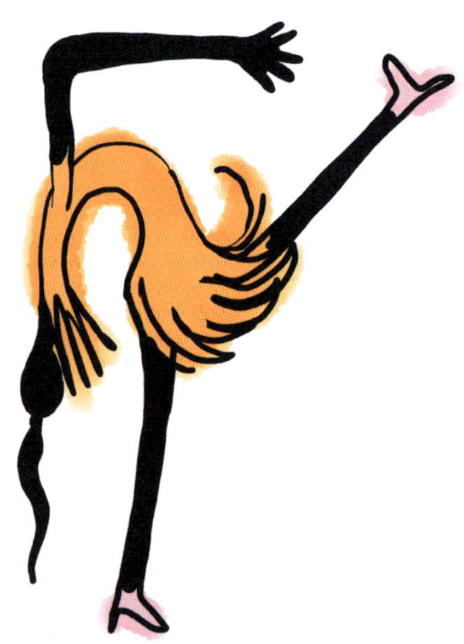

If we can't answer that question then we shouldn't be surprised when governments marginalise the arts and humanities in education, or when the 'brighter' students are directed away from the arts and into science and tech, or when support for theatres, libraries and concert halls is the first thing to be withdrawn in a financial squeeze.

If the arts are seen as just a pretty luxury – the dessert, not the meal – then those decisions make a kind of sense.

So why do we engage in these activities we call art? People say things like; art helps me see the world, art helps me understand the world, art helps me imagine new worlds, art helps me to escape, connect, relax, energise, forget, remember, heal, disrupt, recognise, resist, forgive, accept, change . . .

But what do they mean? How does it actually work? How can listening to a piece of music, for example, do any of those things?

This book is an attempt to answer those questions. It's the beginning of a theory of art.

As short and simple as possible, it begins to answer the questions:

What does art do?
And why do we need it?

Why do I, for example, like one set of colours more than another?

Why do I wear my hair like this but never like that?

Why do I prefer oak furniture to pine?

Why do I like this dance but not that one?

**Why do I
want to
listen to
one specific record again
and again
and again
and again
and again
and again**

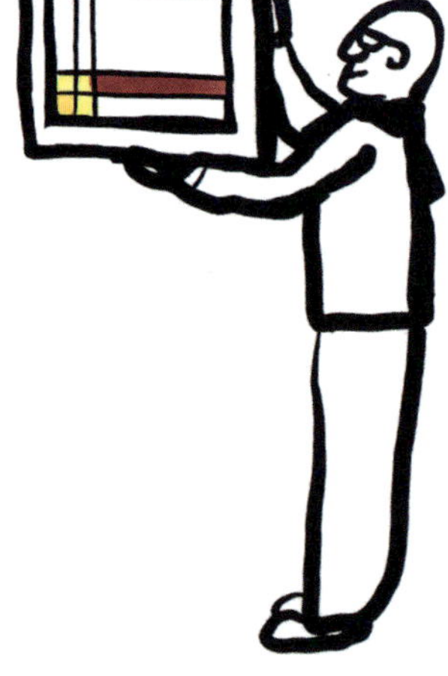

art

Let's start with that word.

What does it mean?

In this book the word 'art' is used in the broadest sense possible. It includes all the expected things like:

novels
sculptures
symphonies
albums
paintings
films
ballets
plays
poems
operas . . .

BUT WE'LL ALSO USE

COCKTAILS . GANGNAM STYLE . CARPETS . TALL TALES . GARDENS . KNITTE
CARDS . MASCARA . TRAINERS . CROCKERY . CAKE DECORATION . SOAP OPER
. KITES . TATTOOS . PICTURE FRAMES . BIRDWATCHING . FALSE BREASTS . P.
HEELS . DAD JOKES . BALLOONS . DOING IMPRESSIONS . PRODUCT DESIGN . S
STONES . JUGGLING . FORTUNE TELLING . ESCAPOLOGY . FLEA CIRCUSES .
POLISH . HATS . SKIPPING . BRAIDS . WEDDING DRESSES . SELFIES . FAKE FR
CAN LABELS . KEY CHAINS . RIVER DANCE . WORDPLAY . TREE TOPPERS . DO
SKATE BOARDS . PENJING . SCARIFICATION . TOOTH FILING . GOSPEL . THERI
NAMES . CORSAGES . MOSAICS . TIES . NICKNAMES . LIPOSUCTION . POMP
TEMPLES . JINGLES . JUJU HATS . NEEDLEWORK . HEADDRESSES . MOON
JOKES . MAKING THE BED . SHOE SHINING . MIXING COLOURS . LIPSTICKS .
. PATTY CAKE . PATTERNS . CLASPS . CORSETS . PLUMES . DIAMOND CUT
AUTOMATA . SEASHELL CRAFT . CLOWNS . RUGELACH . AQUARIA . DOOR HAN
. VAMPIRES . SILVERWARE . CLOGS . CALL OF DUTY . BAKLAVA . TWERKING .
. NIGHTGOWNS . CHANDELIERS . OBELISKS . FORMALWEAR . QUILTS . DOLMA
. KAFTANS . HORROR STORIES . SPAGHETTI STRAPS . ALTARS . BROOCHES .
SPELL . BREAKDANCING . KUFIS . VIDEOGAMES . STRIPED SHIRTS . COSMET
. ZOMBIES . BARBIES . LOUNGEWEAR . LYRICS . ARCHITECTURE . COUNTRY S
GOBLETS . EROTICA . SUNCATCHERS . WINKING . BLANKET FORTS . PENTAGO
. LUTES . BUCKLES . HASHTAGS . HOPAK . DRUMS . FOLDING . COFFINS . AL
MINIATURES . PAPIER-MÂCHÉ . TIARAS . SHADOW PLAY . KIMONOS . MULLET
. HYDRAULOPHONES . CHAMPAGNE FLUTES . CUFFLINKS . FAUX FUR . GLIT
. FONTS . DOLLS . PERGOLAS . GILDING . WIND CHIMES . ETCHING . HEADE
ICONOGRAPHY . HAIR TRANSPLANTS . STORYTELLING . ASTROLOGY . CREAT
GUITARS . SWINGS . MOTTOS . CUFFS . WATER SLIDES . THEME PARKS . LAR
TASTING . SUGAR ARTISTRY . RESTAURANT REVIEWS . TURBANS . PILLARS
. NOSE RINGS . MONOGRAMS . LEGOS . NATIONAL ANTHEMS . MUSICALS
PATTERNS . SILK SCREEN PRINTING . MANTRAS . AROMATHERAPY . KINETIC
. PORTRAITS . SARONGS . ENGRAVED PENS . PAGODAS . FLIPBOOKS . ROSAI
. INCENSE . TWIRLING . RUGS . GARDENING . DECANTERS . BUNTING . CAPE
MAGIC TRICKS . BANJOS . IMPERSONATIONS . GEOCACHING . QUILLING . STO
SEASONING . ICE BUCKETS . HEARTS . MOTIFS . HAIRBANDS . PATCHWORK . CE
. COMICS . HORAH . POLE DANCING . TYPOGRAPHY . COASTERS . CLOCK FAC
KNITTING . PRINTMAKING . TILES . COLLAGES . DIORAMAS . PINHOLE PHOTO
. HULA HOOPS . FELTING . GLASSBLOWING . BOWS . VIOLINS . MONTAGE . N
SCREENSAVERS . INSTALLATIONS . TEA COSIES . SUNGLASSES . SWIRLS . C
TREES . WEREWOLVES . TALISMANS . FLAGS . COOKING . SCRAPBOOKING . TR
BUNRAKU . CARD TRICKS . SAND ART . STOP MOTION . BRAIDING . DOLLHOUS
. ANIMATION . STENCILS . TRIANGLES . NIGHT SKY PHOTOGRAPHY . PENMAN

IT TO TALK ABOUT...

NS . JITTERBUG . MOHAWKS . CUPCAKES . SLANG . POP SONGS . BIRTHDAY
LERY . MIME . FOUNTAINS . STAMP COLLECTIONS . HUMMING . BOOK COVERS
NGERIE . EMBROIDERY . BABOUCHES . FUNNY WALKS . WHISTLING . KITTEN
LLOWING . KARAOKE . LACE . FACIAL EXPRESSIONS . PUPPETS . ARRANGING
. CREATIVE CODING . SPOILERS . WALLPAPER . MARBLES . STUCCO . NAIL
NGS . EASTER EGGS . BEADWORK . GRILLS . CUSTOM LICENCE PLATES . SOUP
VE . DAYDREAMING . HENNA . CALLIGRAPHY . KOI PONDS . FIGURE SKATING .
OS . BASKETRY . MASKS . IMPROV . WREATHS . HAIKU . FAIRYTALES . BRAND
ANS . FOOTBALL CHANTS . FLAMENCO . DRESSAGE . POODLE GROOMING .
DRAPERY . RIDDLES . GEMSTONES . DESSERTS . PERFUMERY . PRACTICAL
XTENSIONS . BATTLE RAP . POPPING . TURFING . GARNISH . SLOW DANCING
DERMY . KILTS . SCENTED CANDLES . ILLUMINATION . FORTUNE COOKIES .
ORICE . MERRY-GO-ROUNDS . COTTON CANDY . TOYS . ACTING . LOVE LETTERS
ADING . DIAMONDS . PANAMA HATS . RIFFING . BABY DOLLS . WIGS . RITUALS
BS . LOAFERS . JELLY BEANS . SLINGBACKS . PIÑATAS . WHEEL OF FORTUNE
ING . LIMERICKS . BOW TIES . SIDEBURNS . THEATRE CURTAINS . CASTING A
KITCHEN TILES . POTTED PLANTS . WEDDING RINGS . MELODIES . PERFUME
RMAIDS . STAINED GLASS . POLKA DOTS . EPIC POETRY . STREET PARTIES .
ORATING . ROLE PLAYING . DJING . GIVING A TOAST . COLLECTING MEMENTOS
HIP-HOP . MODELLING . HAIR GEL . MYTHS . ORIGAMI . BATIK . BRACELETS .
S . EMBELLISHING . MANDALAS . LEDERHOSEN . GHOSTS . TEA CEREMONIES
ANNING . CORNROWS . BAY WINDOWS . SEE-SAWS . WELCOME DOORMATS
LITHOGRAPHY . BRASS FINISHING . TOE RINGS . BELLY DANCING . HYMNS .
G . COLOURED INDEX CARDS . COLOUR THEORY . TUTUS . UNICYCLES . BASS
ZES . POLISHING . TAROT READING . CENTERPIECES . REELS . NOOKS . WINE
LANTS . MOCKTAILS . COOKING SHOWS . MEMOIRS . JIVING . CONTOURING
CING . VINTAGE FAUCETS . QUIPS . ZINES . YODELLING . MANHOLE COVER
S . CRYSTAL COLLECTING . GRAVESTONES . ACTION PAINTING . PATAPHYSICS
IDOSCOPES . SEAMS . CLOAKS . CANDLE MAKING . METALWORK . MARKERS
LPTURES . CONCERTOS . CARTOONS . MANGA . SKETCHING . UPHOLSTERY .
NG . WREATH MAKING . SKIRTING BOARDS . FLOWERPOTS . SALT SHAKERS .
URTAINS . MATCHSTICK MODELS . TERRARIUMS . VIDEO EDITING . ENGRAVING
NDS . ARABESQUES . WISECRACKS . SOAP MAKING . STICKERS . POSTERS .
PHORISMS . SONGWRITING . JUMP ROPE . MIRRORS . CALAVERA . DOODLING
LWAYS . PLASTICINE . HAIRSTYLES . PAPER CRAFTS . SHADES . PROVERBS .
FRESCOES . POP ART . ANECDOTES . WOODWORKING . UPCYCLING . BONSAI
S . MACRAMÉ . BOOK BINDING . FACE PAINTING . DREAMCATCHERS . STAMPS .
S . TASSEL MAKING . BELL TOLLING . COSTUMES . BOOKMARKS . FURNITURE
NGS . SIGHTSEEING . HARMONICAS . ARCADES . UNICORNS . BOBBY PINS . .

. . . all kinds of things where somebody does more than is absolutely necessary for the sake of the feeling they get by doing it.

WE HAVE TO	WE DON'T HAVE TO
GATHER FOOD	ADD SPRINKLES
EAT & DRINK	DESIGN SILVERWARE
CONSTRUCT SHELTER	HANG WALLPAPER
COMMUNICATE	DO IMPROV
MAINTAIN BODY	DO BODYBUILDING

There are things we have to do to stay alive – like eat food, drink liquid, wear clothes, make money, communicate with each other. And then on top of those things we do thousands of other things that we don't have to do:

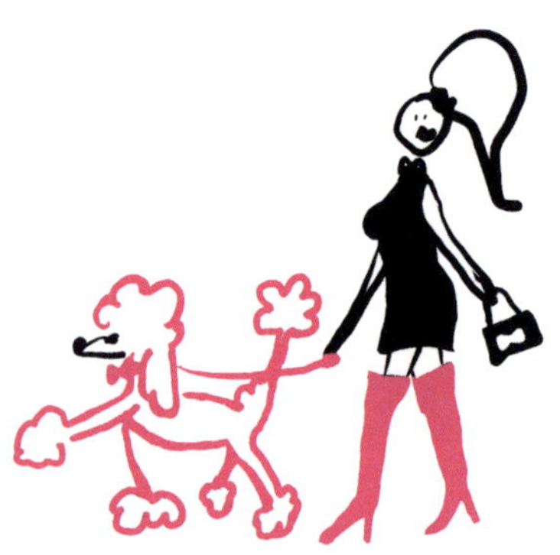

we **embroider** our clothes

we **decorate** our food

we **compose** poems

we **arrange** flowers

we **mix** colours

we **play** instruments

we **invent** slang

we **adorn** our bodies

we **curate** exhibitions

we **sing** and

we **dance** and

we **hum** and

we **drum** . . .

None of those things are necessary, but we punctuate our lives with them. We like the feelings they arouse.

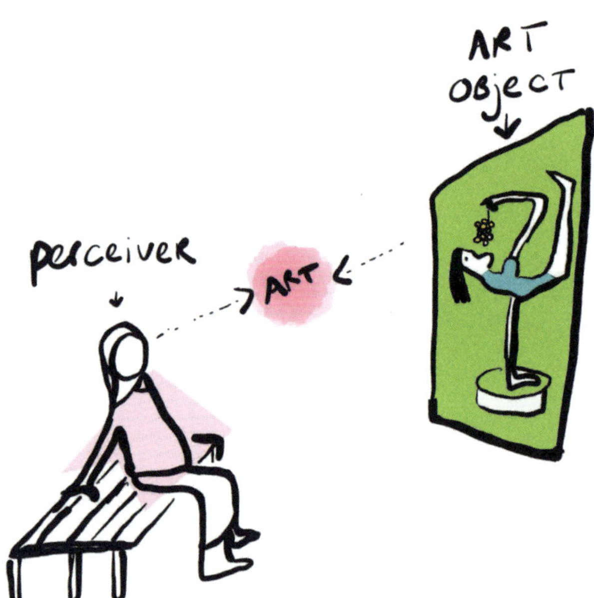

perceiver
ART
ART
OBJECT

we all make art
all the time
but we don't usually
call it that

Artists are people who've decided to make a job of it. Every time somebody puts on their make-up, chooses their jewellery and clothes, dances this way or that, puts on a record, art is being made.

When we speak of an art object we mean 'something that is intended to trigger some feelings'. Art is not a substance that radiates out of paintings or symphonies. Art is a name we give to a certain type of experience. It's the name for a kind of engagement we have with something.

What type of engagement is an art engagement? To understand this, let's think about screwdrivers.

A screwdriver has two parts: the blade and the handle. The blade can really only be made in one form: it has a specific purpose and it has to be a specific shape and size and strength. You couldn't make it out of marble or glass or chocolate. It wouldn't be able to turn a screw. If you go to a hardware store and look at a selection of flat screwdrivers you'll see that all the blades are virtually identical.

This is not true for the handles. There is no space for 'art' in the blades – but there is in the handles, which might be striped or speckled or multicoloured or opaque.

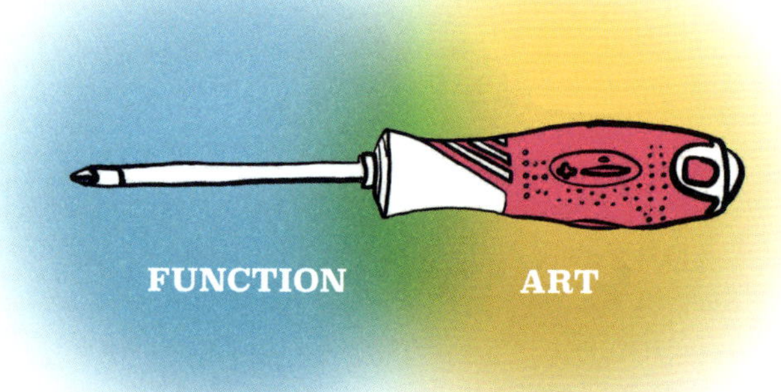

These variations in the handles make no difference to the usability of the tools. They are stylistic variations that don't relate to function.

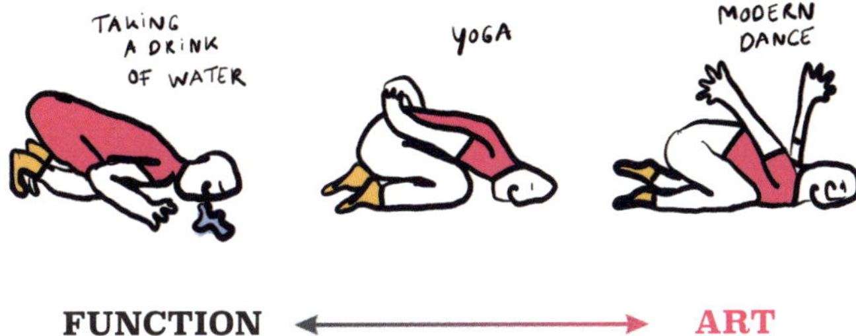

The less functional a thing is – the less it has to do something in particular – the more space for art there is in it; the more freedom there is in it.

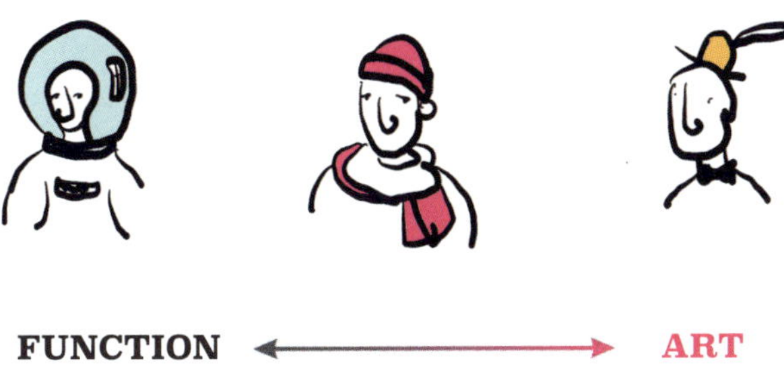

The art engagement begins where the functional engagement ends.

If you're designing a cup that you intend people to be able to drink from, it has to be able to hold liquid; a perforated cup won't work, even if it is very beautifully perforated.

The degrees of freedom in what you do with your cup are limited by the fact that it has a real world use: it has to carry liquid and it has to be drinkable from.

If, on the other hand, you're Grayson Perry or Carol McNicoll, making cups as art objects, there are no restrictions of that kind. You can make the cup any shape you want with as many holes in it as you like, you can paint it with any material you like. You are not expecting anybody to drink from such a cup.

Because it doesn't have a real-world use, it isn't constrained. It has a lot of space for art.

Art can always be otherwise.

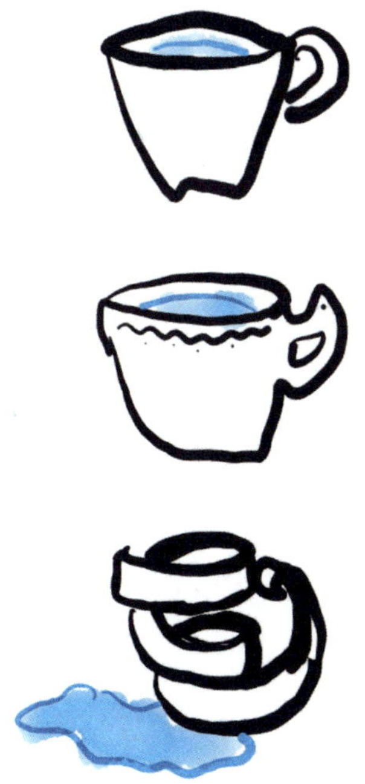

Art only happens where there is room for options, where things can be fundamentally otherwise. An 'EXIT' sign in a theatre exists to indicate as clearly as possible the way out. It has to do that as unambiguously – as unartistically – as possible. A 'FIRE EXIT' sign in pretty swirly colours with a strange typeface wouldn't be a good idea. The more specific the job, the less room for art.

Many activities are part-art, part-function. Running for the bus can't be otherwise – you don't want to miss the bus. But a little playful skip while getting on, can make it part-art.

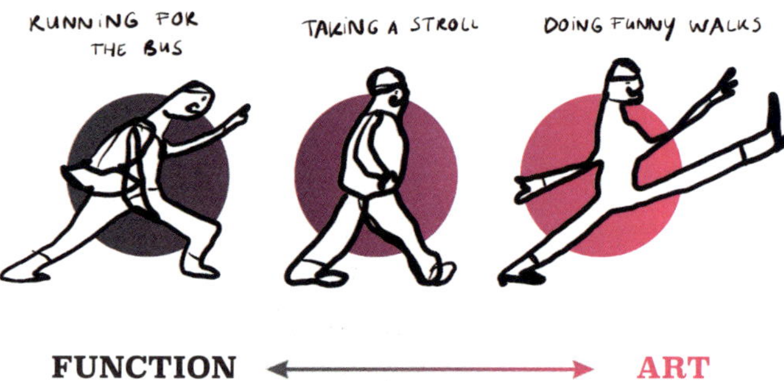

A joke the bus driver makes as she announces the stops, a bird tattoo poking out from under her uniform sleeve, a little movement of her shoulder when she thinks of her favourite song – these are little expressions of art.

The fact that something is generally seen as an art object does not dictate that we will have an art engagement with it.

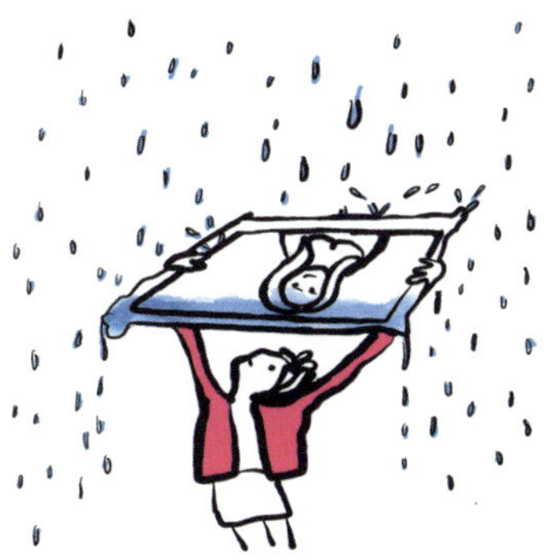

And the fact that something is generally seen as a functional object does not dictate that we can't have an art engagement with it.

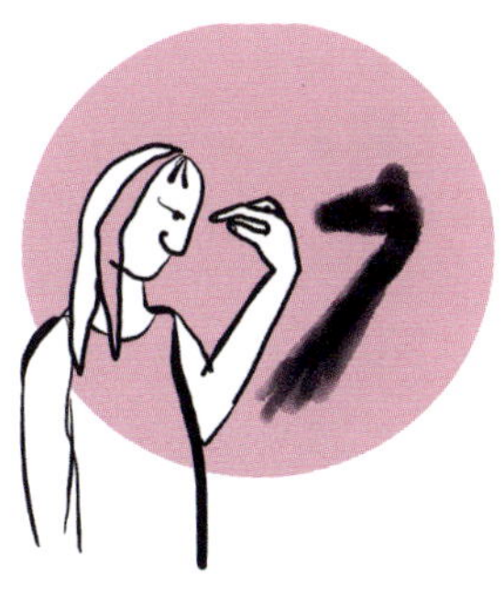

A jar works well if it's plain and simple, but we have made jars in elaborate shapes and forms for millennia.

A plain T-shirt does its job just fine, but we love T-shirts with pictures on them.

And although bare walls keep our roofs up and intruders out, we enjoy hanging paintings on them.

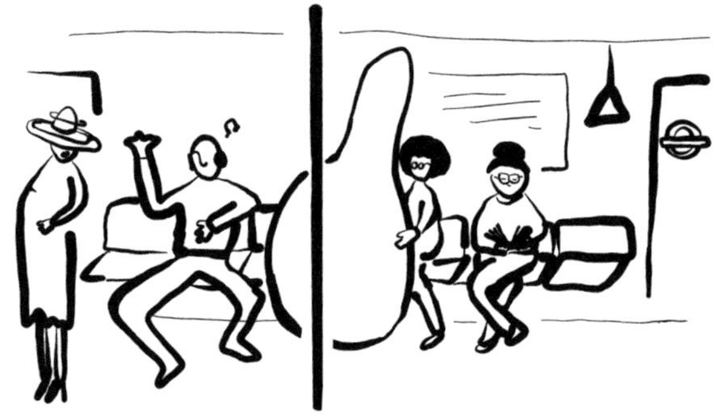

why do we spend our **time** on these **non-functional** activities we call **art?**

Here's a simple idea:

ART IS A WAY OF MAKING FEELINGS HAPPEN

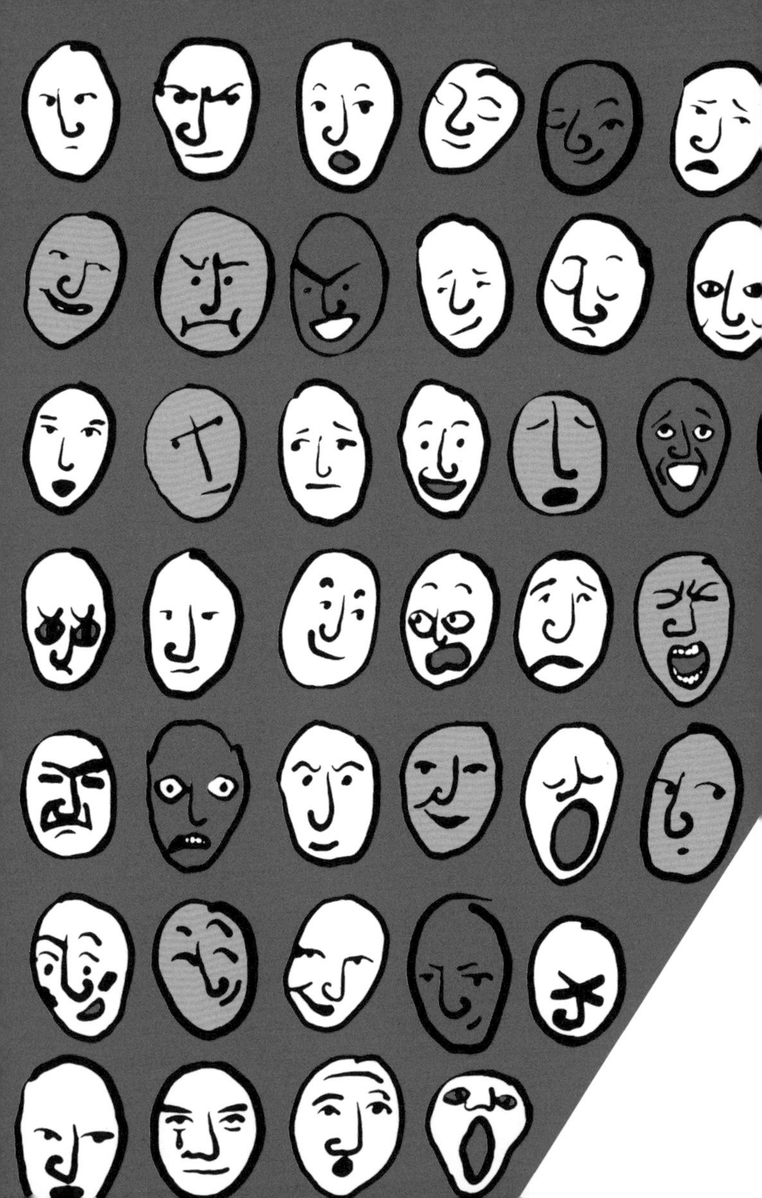

2
feelings

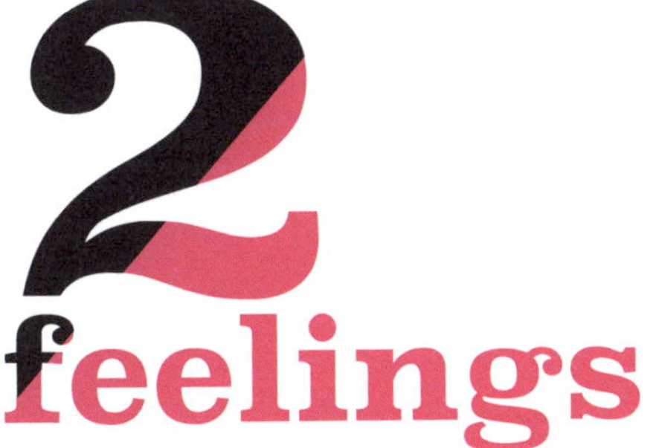

Feelings have a bad reputation.

If you say that as an artist you think your job is to create feelings, other artists – and even more so critics – may look at you a bit askance. It sounds so trivial, so unimportant. Surely, art is more important than that? It may sound trivial, until you realise that what we call feelings comes before what we call cognition – thinking.

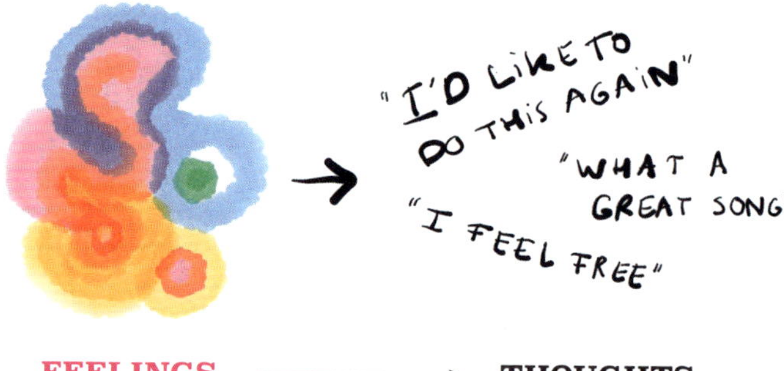

FEELINGS ⟶ **THOUGHTS**

Feelings come before thought and articulation. They are our antennae, they help us feel our way forward into the future.

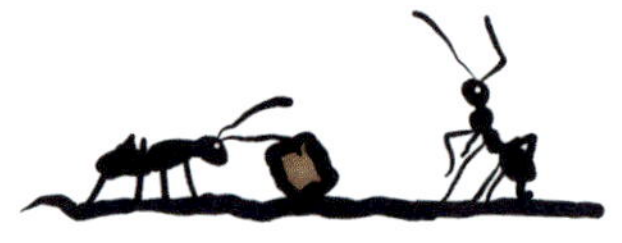

Feelings are faster (and sometimes completely wrong). Logic and deduction are slower (and also sometimes completely wrong!). Faced with a novel situation that needs a quick reaction, we rely primarily on our fast feelings to navigate.

Most of the really big choices in our lives – who to marry, who to vote for, which job to take, whether or not to try to have children – aren't based on just the careful application of logic and deduction: we use our feelings.

It's quite rare in life to have all the information we need to make a perfectly logical assessment, but nevertheless we can't stand still: we often need to make decisions before the evidence has been collected and weighed.

'Emotions play a fundamental role in survival.'

MARK SOLMS, neuropsychologist

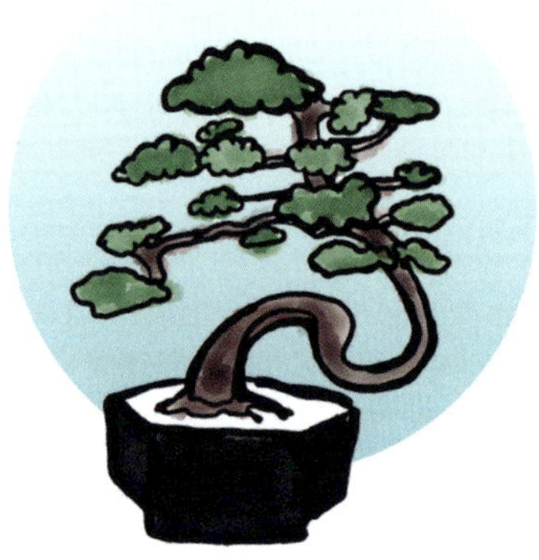

Feelings are known as fuzzy, hard to pin down, impossible to measure and ever changing. In a technical culture like Western culture, things you can't count, don't count.

Of course, there do exist ways of making decisions that are not based on feelings. They have to do with deduction and data. Those are usually grouped under the heading of Science.

Science works by clearing the ground around a topic – by removing extraneous details and trying to isolate what is intended to be studied, so we can watch the behaviour of just one thing in isolation. As much as possible, science wants to remove all feelings from the scene: the outcome of an experiment shouldn't depend on whether the experimenter is having a bad day or is a Catholic. That is the essence of testability – that when you do the same experiment I'm doing, you get the same result I got. From that kind of universality we can make reliable predictive statements about things and build tools that work.

In most of our life we often can't separate things out as clearly as that. Our situations, our fears, our desires, our values – they're all bound up together, and we only have one life, one chance to see what works and what doesn't. And it's all in motion too.

We need to use our hunches, our guesses, our gut.

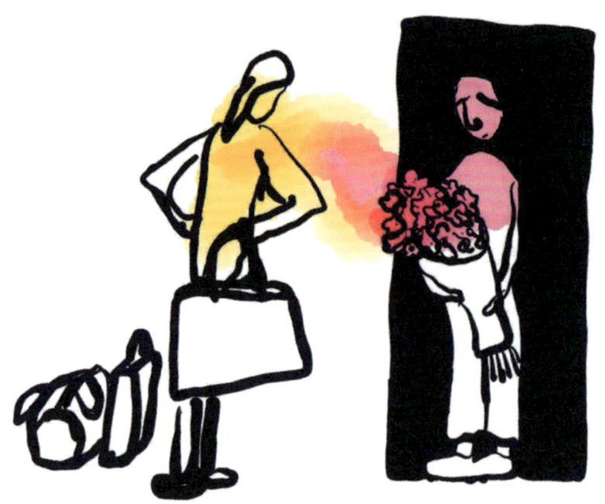

Feelings are not rational, but there is some logic to how we deal with them. We have a whole lifetime of experience in feelings, and we learn how to recognise them and what value to give to them. We weigh our feelings against our past experiences.

Children will often fear the dark but as they grow up they usually accept that there aren't unseen monsters waiting for them, and they learn to ignore the feeling (though it can easily be re-aroused – for example by horror films and haunted houses).

Because we know that feelings are subjective and personal, we are prepared to revise them – like when somebody you first thought was a bit strange becomes your best friend.

Feelings are powerful precisely because they aren't articulated.

Advertisers and product designers know how to create feelings around something, so that they connect with you on an emotional level. Adding an aromatic chemical like Calone to washing powder can ignite associations with the ozonic smell of the seaside, and connects to feelings of 'fresh' and 'clean'.

In the right context, using very high-contrast photos of people makes them look like criminals – because we associate such pictures with police 'wanted' images. That gets reinforced by early black-and-white film, where the villains and monsters are always high contrast – while the 'goodies' get Vaseline-lensed.

The feelings generated by art aren't always nice feelings, but they won't hurt you. When encountering Hannibal Lecter you might not be having nice feelings – it's a terrifying character! But you might enjoy being terrified . . .

How does that work?

it works because art is **harmless,** because art is a **fiction**

Art is of no inescapable consequence.

ART IS ESCAPABLE

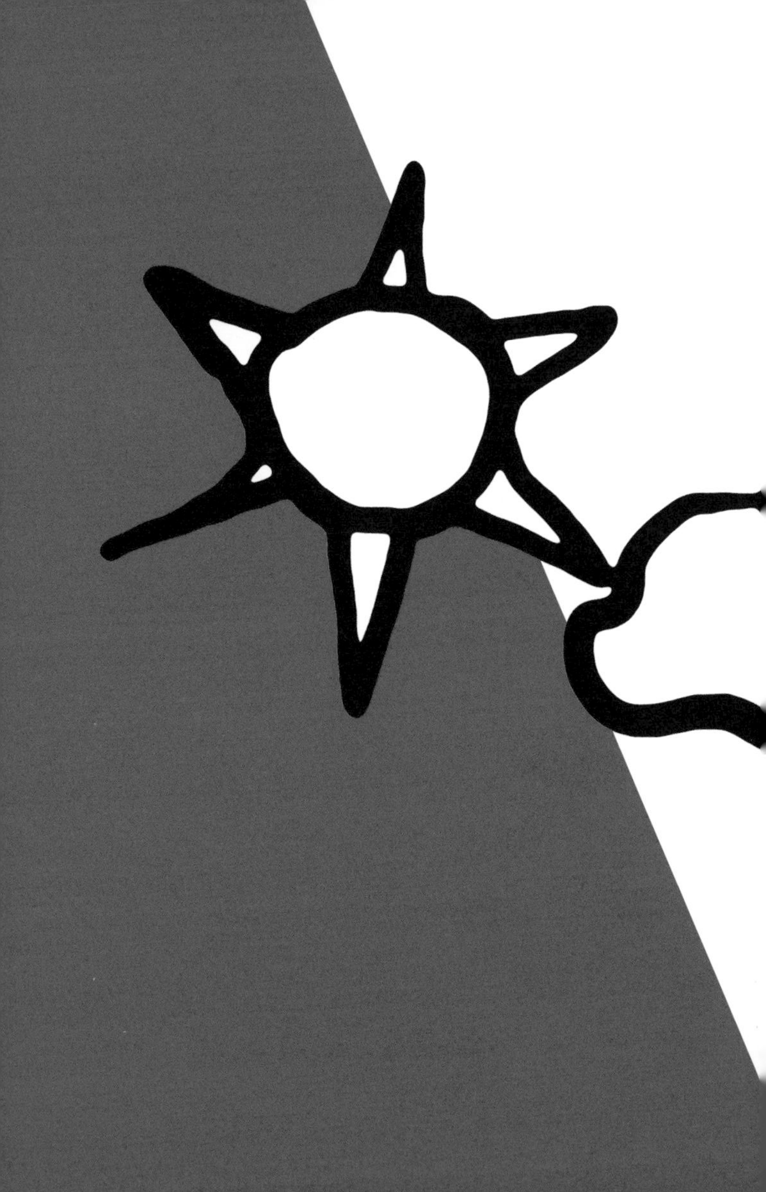

3

fiction
feelings

Humans have this strange quirk of enjoying feelings through fictions . . . being 'frightened' during a game of hide-and-seek, being 'tantalised' by a description of a long-lingering kiss in a poem, being 'upset' by the deceptive actions of a character in a soap opera.

We can experience the heartbreak of a character in a movie – but at a safe distance that turns it from real heartbreak into a feeling we can enjoy.

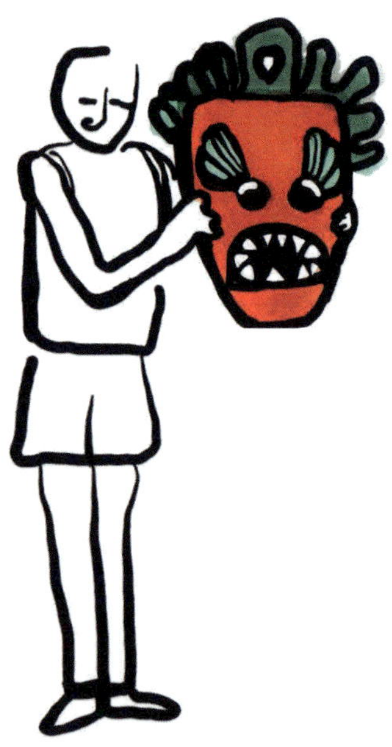

There are many examples of art changing the course of history, advancing revolutions, bringing stone-cold people to tears and horrifying conservative parents.

Art can have a tremendous effect on the world – that is why dictators have been so eager to lock artists away or employ them as propagandists.

but art is **effective** **because** it is **safe**

You can read a novel and experience the horror of a prison or the beauty of deep love – but you don't have to endure the real-world consequences of those things.

You can shut the book. You can leave the gallery. You can stop dancing, close your eyes, exit the movie theatre.

You can go away and you can get back to your life.

But you can take with you some memory of the feelings you had and that can change *you*.

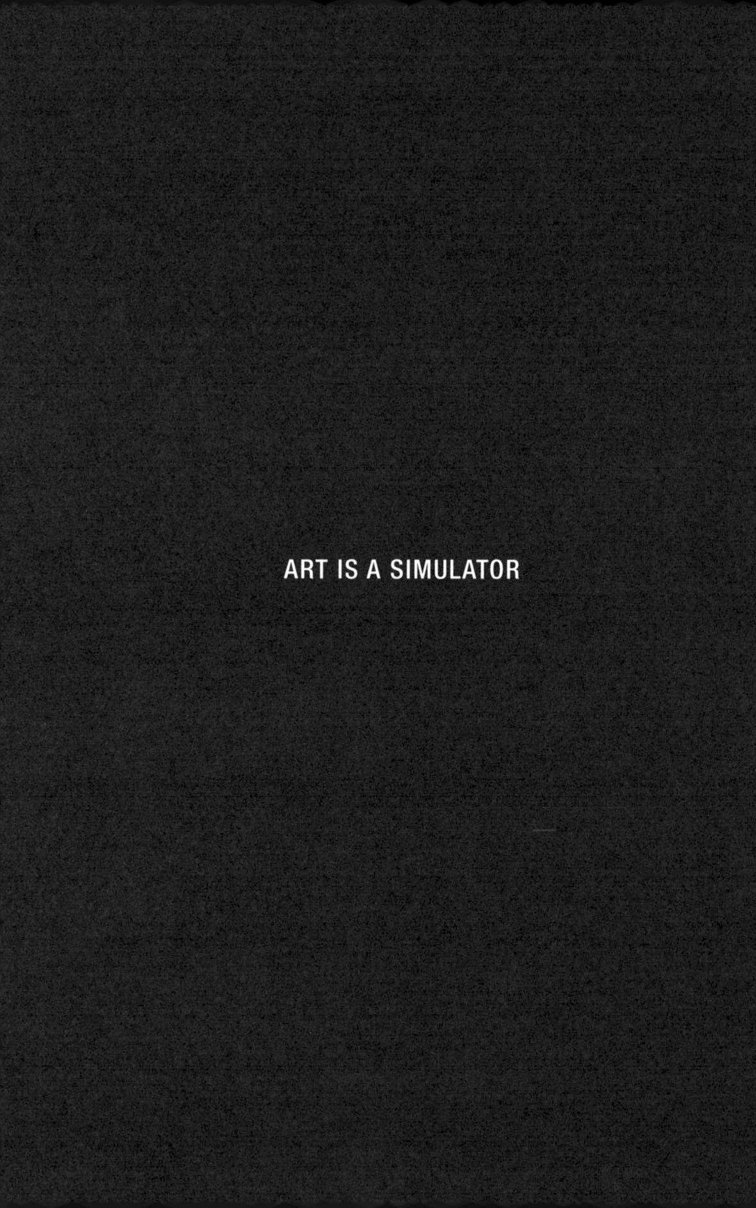ART IS A SIMULATOR

Think of a flight simulator, which is what pilots practise in. You have all the experiences of flying the plane, but you never leave the ground. But the feelings feel real. You feel elated when you take off successfully and you sweat anxiously as you try to bring the plane in for a tidy landing.

What would the name for feelings of that kind be? Artificial feelings? Virtual feelings?

Fiction feelings?

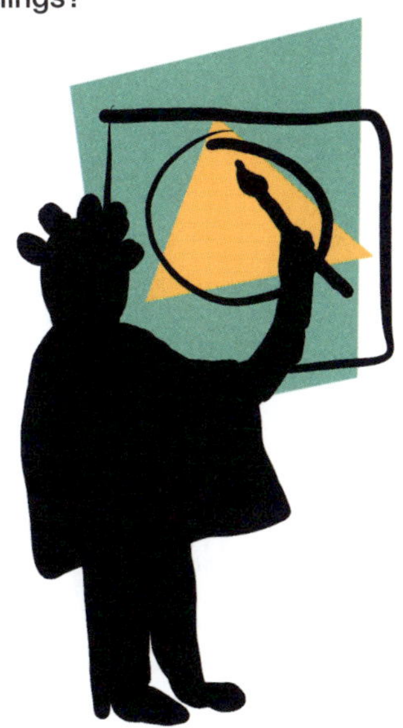

What's the point of fiction feelings?

They alert you to the range of feelings you are capable of having. They enrich your feelings repertoire. They tell you something about other possible worlds: those you might want to be in, and those you might want to avoid.

They tell you those things in advance of ever encountering them . . . so you have a repertoire of feelings about 'fictional worlds' in your mind. And in these fictional worlds you are allowed to take the consequences as seriously and non-seriously as you want.

The level of seriousness is entirely up to you.

REAL ("HAS CONSEQUENCES YOU CAN'T ESCAPE")	**FICTION** ("OF NO INESCAPABLE CONSEQUENCE")
WAR	A POEM ABOUT WAR
NOT HAVING SHOES	NOT HAVING SHOE-TASSELS
FINDING OUT ABOUT YOUR REAL FATHER	FINDING OUT ABOUT DARTH VADER

(Sometimes we get so attached to fictional worlds that they become our reality, and they are no longer playful and harmless. For instance, when many people believe in a fiction and start adjusting their expectations and behaviour as though it is true, thereby bringing it into being. Or when a large part of someone's life takes place in a fictional game and the developments in that game truly impact them. These fictional worlds become like reality to us, and then we make fictional worlds about those, virtualisations of virtualisations, and virtualisations of those – until everyone has forgotten where it all began. (Conspiracy theories are perhaps games gone wrong.))

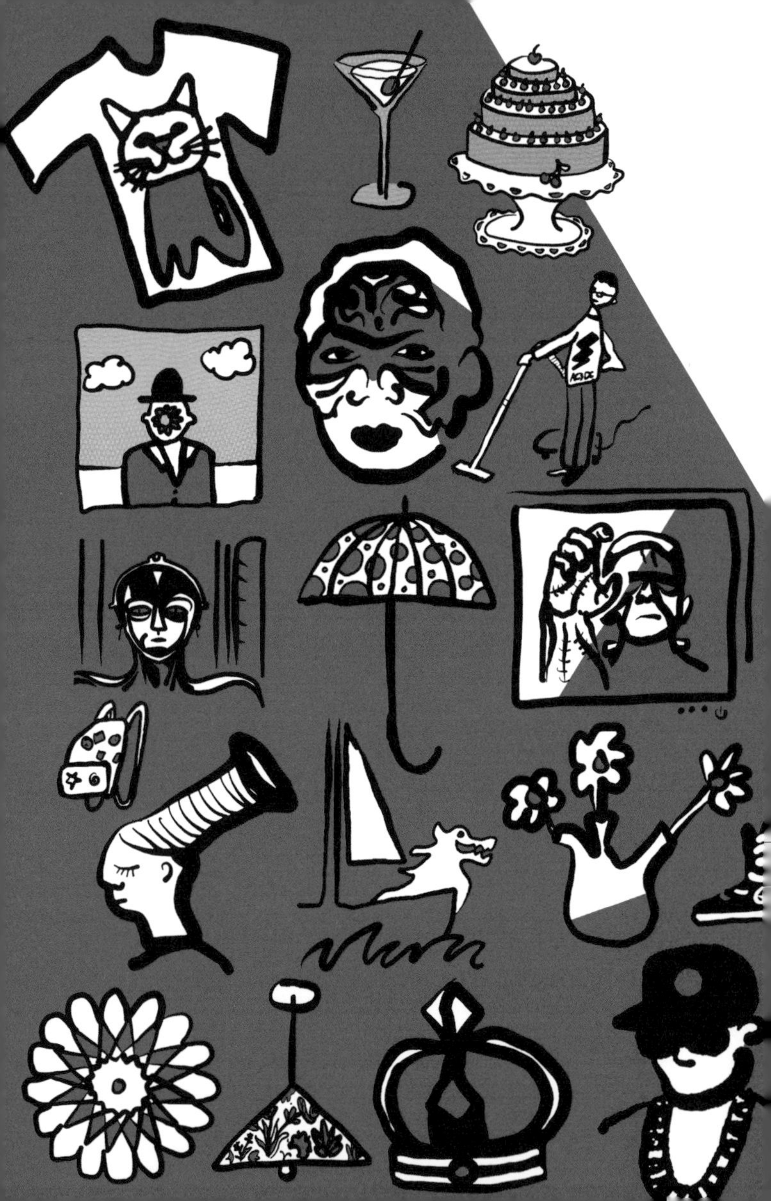

fictional worlds

4

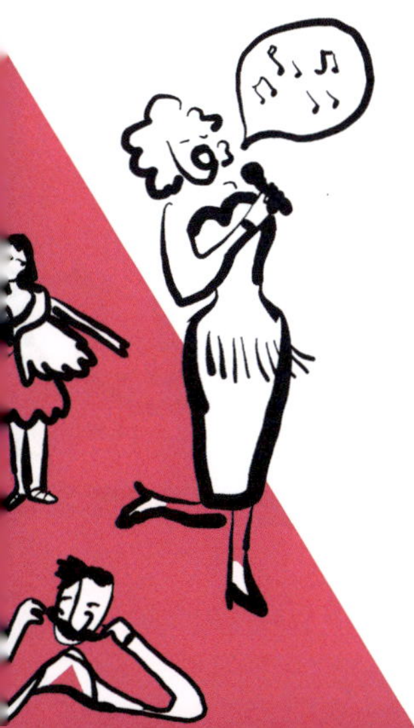

We humans are extremely receptive to world-making. We need only very little information and in the right context we can make huge leaps of the imagination, extrapolating that information to an entire world.

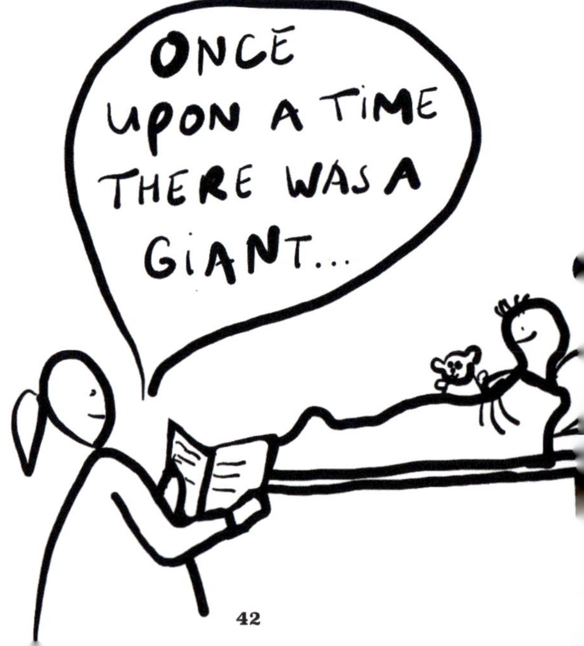

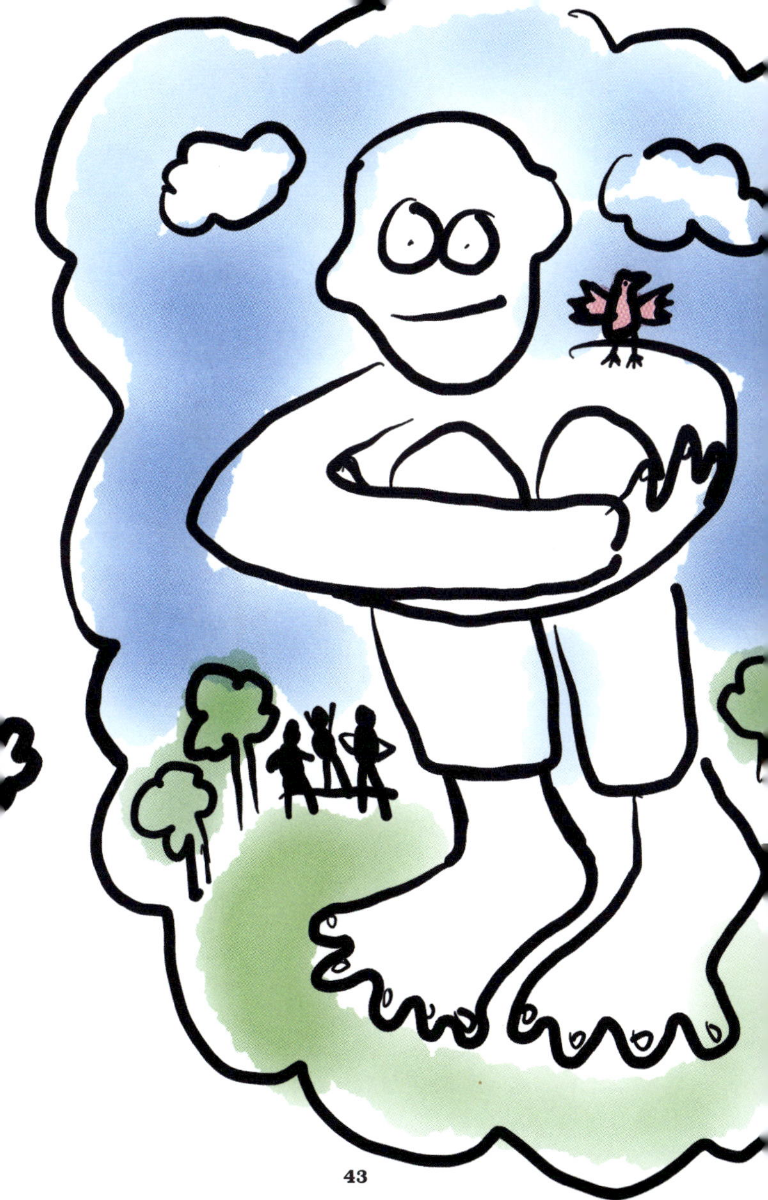

We already carry with us a huge amount of experience that can be extrapolated to possible other worlds, but we don't think about it that much.

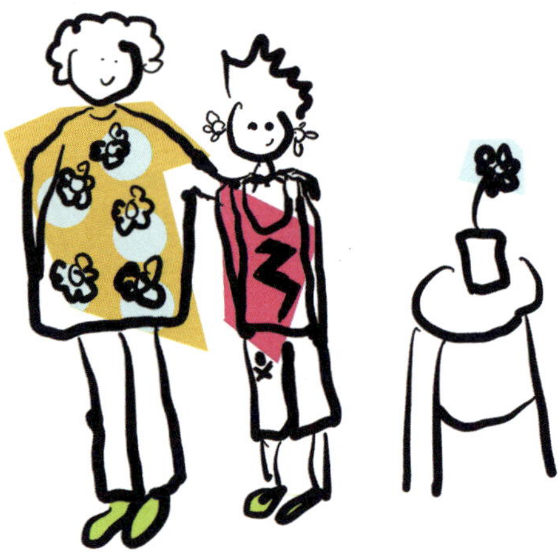

We carry, for example, 'Bauhaus World', 'Laura Ashley World', '*1984* World', 'AC/DC World', 'Pokémon World' . . . and a thousand others.

Some of them might be quite personal, only shareable with a few others, like a secret handshake with your sister. And some might be quite universal, like a long dress with little flowers on it. This dress can be extrapolated to a possible world . . . a more romantic world, a world where things are nice and gentle.

Most art objects don't describe a whole world in detail like *1984* does. Instead they come only as fragments of another world, and another way of being.

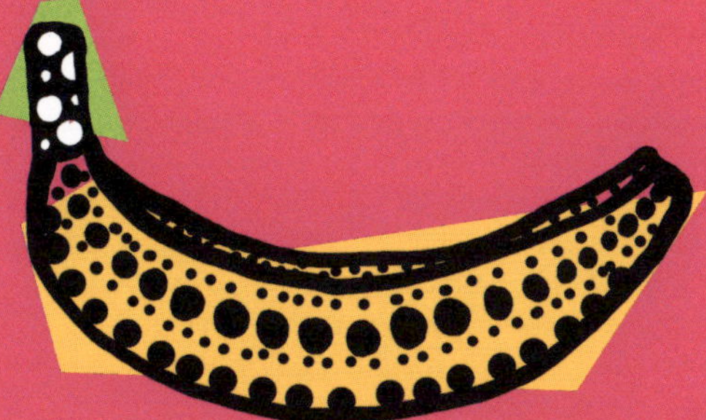

They're like a channel into another universe, or like relics from the future. They're pulled into our current reality as representatives of another possible reality.

Though it's easy to see how a novel like *1984* describes another world or another way of being, it's harder to see how something so small as an earring does that.

How is another world suggested when there is no narrative or explanation involved? Where do we find that message in a small object? How does that work?

Let's start explaining this by asking: what makes you choose one earring over another? You've seen earrings all your life, so when you see a new one, you immediately unconsciously compare it to all the others you've seen. In your history of earring-viewing, how does this one compare?

Is it bigger than any earring you've seen before?

Is it bolder, or more concealed, or more understated? ■ Is it longer? ■ Is it danglie
■ Sparklier? ■ Is it more intricate or simpler? ■ Is it darker or brighter? ■ Ha
colour been added to it or is it the colour of the material? ■ Is it symmetrical
asymmetrical? ■ Slender or bulky? ■ Is it dangling towards the shoulder or climbir
up the auricle? ■ Is it spiky or soft? ■ Is it a figurative form, like a grape, or is it
geometrical form, like a circle? ■ Is it made of something expensive or cheap?
Does the earring cover the earlobe or does it create a visible hole in the earlobe
■ Is it made of one material or several materials combined? ■ Is it shiny or matte
■ Is it made of natural materials, like gold or feathers, or synthetic materials, lil
acrylic beads? ■ Is it made by the person wearing it, or is it made by Cartier?
Does it make a sound when it moves? ■ Is it made of something earrings aren
usually made from – say like cigarette ends or electrical cable? ■ Does it reveal th
designer in an obvious way or in a hidden way that is only known to insiders? ■
it lush or stark? ■ Does it show much of the ear or cover it? ■ Is it easy to put c
or does it require effort? ■ Is the shape familiar or unusual? ■ Is it stately or flashy
■ Is it angular or curved? ■ Does it look heavy or light? ■ Is it intended to loc
expensive or wacky? ■ Does the form have romantic associations, or a businessli
appearance? ■ Is there a symbolic element in the design, like a cross or a sku
■ Is it ironic? ■ Does it match the outfit? ■ Is it demure or brash? ■ Does it loc
comfortable to wear for long periods? ■ Is it trendy or timeless? ■ Is it engrave
or patterned? ■ Does it look unique or mass-produced? ■ Is it delicate or robus
■ Is it gender-specific or unisex? ■ Is it sophisticated or fun? ■ Is it flexible
rigid? ■ Does it attract attention or is it nearly invisible? ■ If it is adorned wi
stones, are they natural or artifical? Precious or semi-precious? ■ Does it conta
a message, like name or a word? ■ Can the earring-wearer easily move the
head? ■ Is the earring covered by hair? ■ Is it possible to do outdoor activitie
like biking or camping, while wearing the earring? ■ Can it be worn in water
should it be kept dry? ■ Is it suitable for all ages or more for a specific age grou
■ Is it likely to snag on clothing? ■ Is it something a grandmother would wear?
Does it catch the light or absorb it? ■ Does it glow in the dark? ■ Is it big enou
to be seen from a distance or only up close? ■ Can it double as a gadget? ■ C
it be mistaken for food? ■ Can it be used to signal aliens? ■ Does it have a
hidden compartments or other secret elements? ■ Is it funny or serious lookin
■ Is it the kind of earring that might start a conversation with a stranger? ■ Is
safe to wear it on public transport? ■ Is it pet-friendly? ■ Is it eco-friendly?
Would it be appropriate for a job interview? ■ Is it traditional looking or rebelliou

There are millions of possibilities, and then all the combinations of them. These differences say something to us, and we earring-viewers register them without even being aware of it. Some of the differences we might like – the colour might remind us of a beach vacation, or that new jagged shape suits our current political direction – and we will choose that one. It is a world that we like. Or it's a world that we don't like, or feel indifferent towards. But we can 'read' these little artworks by noticing all the small choices involved. This usually isn't something we do consciously. It's a feeling that we're acting upon.

It's like finding a fragment of a different world.

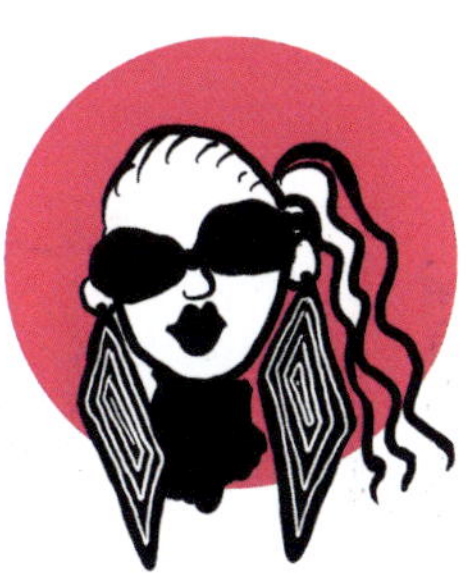

**a more romantic
or more eccentric
or sexier
or earthier
or crazier
or saner
or swashbucklier**

world

'Sometimes you can take the whole of the world in,
and sometimes you need a small piece to take in.
I think that is really what a work of art is: it is a small
piece that you can ingest, that gives you an idea of
the richness of the whole.'

Sister Mary Corita Kent, artist

We all share a history of objects and artworks. When we see a new earring, or any artwork, we look at where this new one sits in our history of looking at artworks. It's like being presented with the latest sentence in a long story. We look for how this artwork chooses to be different from what came before. It's more jagged, or it's more soft, or it's more detailed, or it's less detailed, or it tastes saltier, it smells muskier, it sounds rougher, it feels stickier. Somehow or another, the message is: 'This is a difference that feels interesting today.'

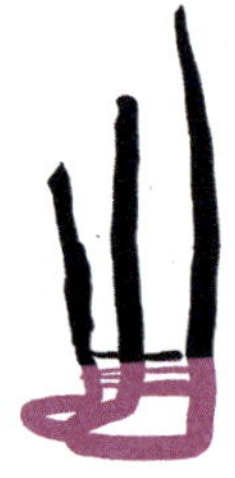 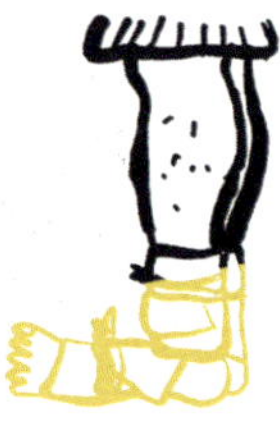 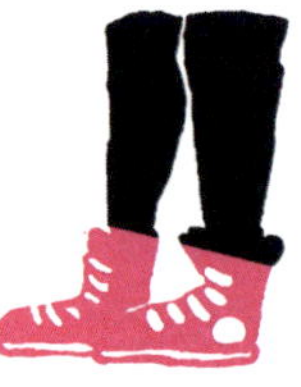 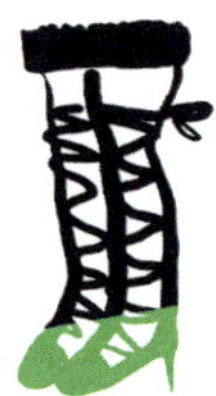

WHEN YOU ARE LOOKING AT ART
YOU ARE LOOKING AT DIFFERENCES

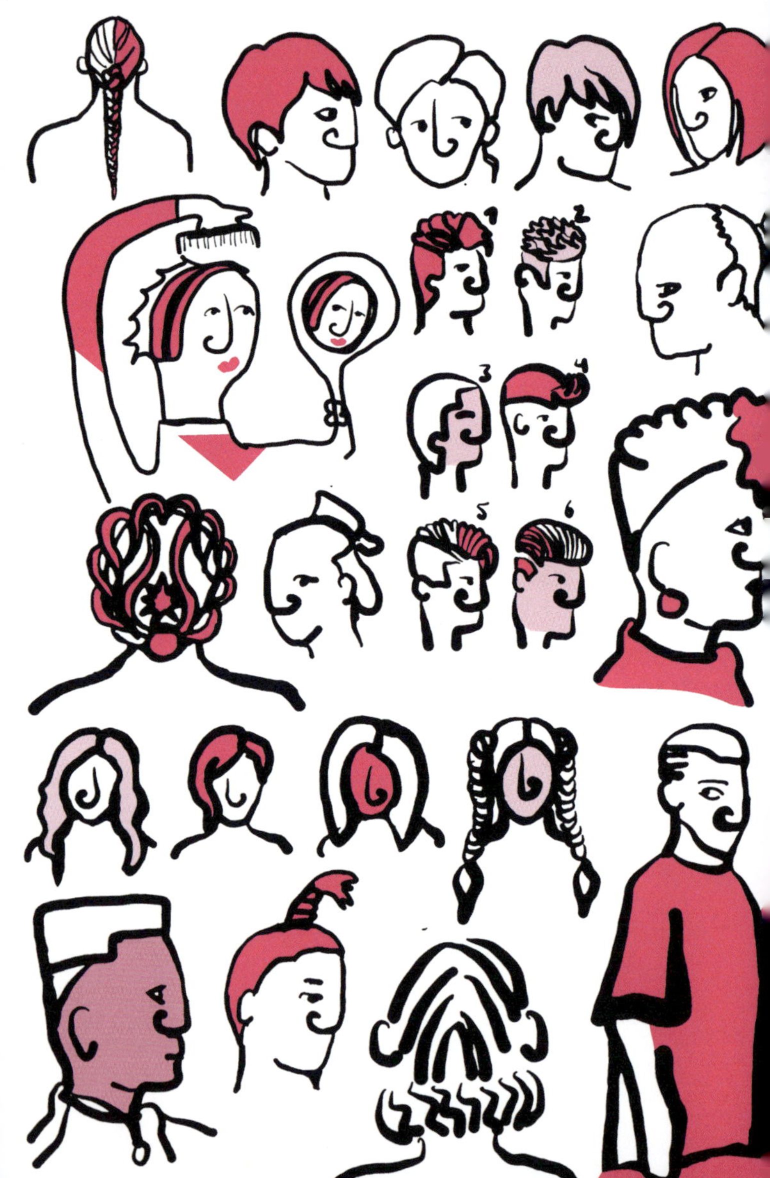

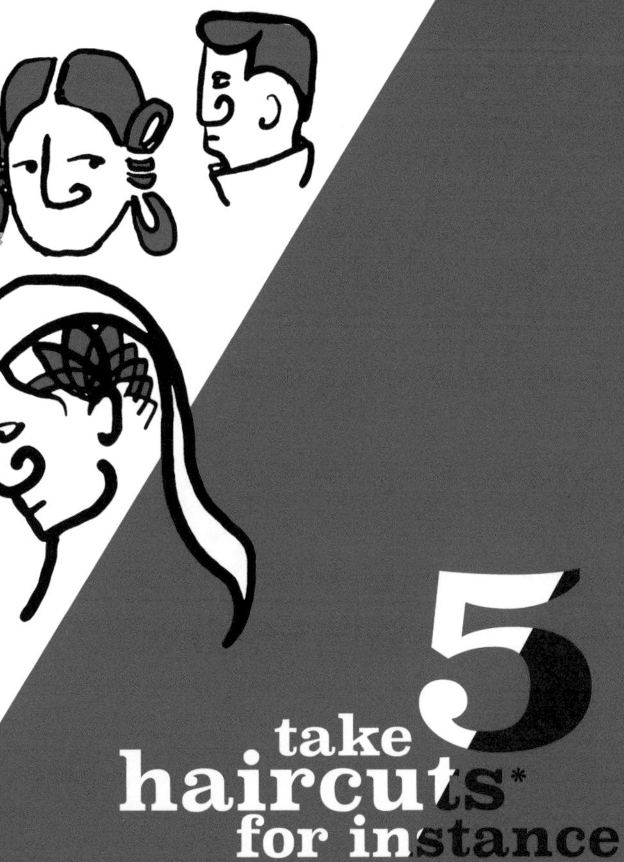

take 5

haircuts*
for instance

* a commonplace
art practice
that most
people
engage
with

Classical art historians tended to believe that artworks are a sort of container for meaning, and that meaning originates in the artist's mind (or the mind of God), and is then transmitted out to the viewer through the object.

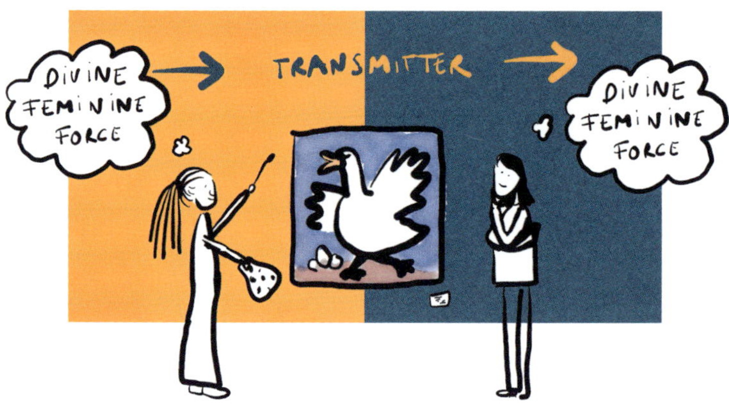

In this view there is a one-way flow: from the artist's imagination into the object and then from the object into the viewer's mind. The art object in that view is a kind of transmitter.

But there is another view: that an art object doesn't have any intrinsic meaning, but is actually a trigger, a way of causing something to happen in your mind.

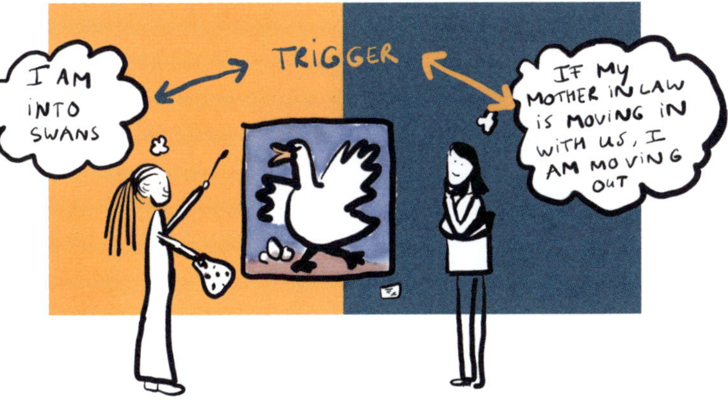

This may not be the same thing that happens in someone else's mind.

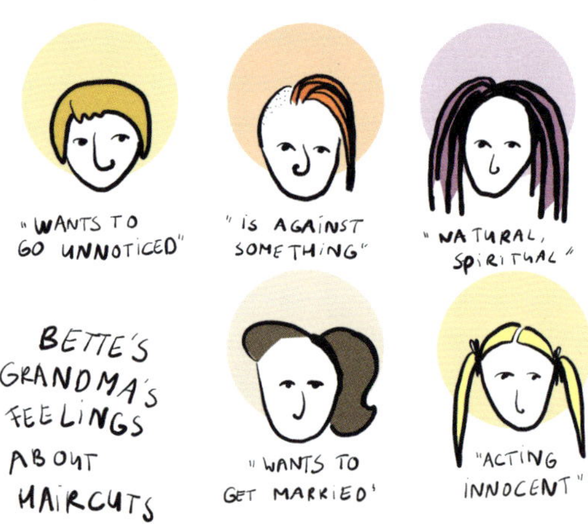

What happens in your mind when you see an artwork depends on your personal history and the history of your culture. It is like a language that changes meaning depending on the listener.

Take haircuts, for instance – the practice of shortening your hair. The very first intentional haircuts in human history may have been simply functional: a way to keep the hair out of your eyes.

And, since humans love experimenting, they would naturally have developed different ways of doing that – some easier, some more elaborate. Perhaps, in some groups, women started doing it differently from men, or older people differently from younger ones. Those different ways of doing it would soon come to stand for 'male or female', 'older or younger'.

A difference might develop between people who kept their hair short and those who decided to let it grow long, which might be a sign that you had lots of spare time on your hands; you didn't work, for example.

All the new ways of cutting hair – new stylings – gather associations. They come to stand for 'rich or poor' or 'high status or low status', 'rebellious or conformist', 'sober or wild' . . .

Quite soon a whole haircut vocabulary develops. Each distinction comes with the heritage of a certain meaning within a certain group. We can imagine these distinctions as axes (plural of axis): lines representing a spectrum you could take a position on.

The very first haircut distinction would be ....

The second one might be ....

The third one might be ....

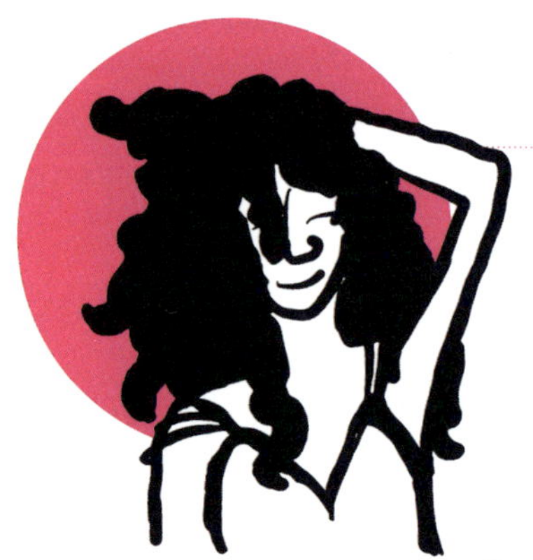

and there are

'NATURAL'

A modern example would be
haircuts that are intended
to look 'natural'. In some
communities, 'natural' might
suggest: 'I have an outdoor
life, perhaps I ride horses or
motor bikes.'

haircut / no haircut.

female / male.

wealthy / poor,

or

powerful / not powerful,

able to get hold of resources / not able to.

(It doesn't matter what the sequence is really.)

many others . . .

At the other extreme of that
axis (we could call it the
'natural / stylised' axis) we
might find the highly sculpted
beehive haircut – a construction
that suggests time, formality,
maintenance.

'STYLISED'

When you choose a haircut you will probably be choosing a point somewhere along that 'natural / stylised' axis. But that isn't the only axis: you might also be operating on the 'conformist / rebellious' axis, on the 'feminine / masculine' axis, on the 'retro / futuro' axis. There are many. Once you start overlaying these axes, one on top of the other, you start to see the sum of all the distinctions you have (consciously or unconsciously) taken a position on.

You are using this haircut as a sort of surrogate version of you . . . or a you that you might want to try out for a while.

It's a way of saying:

'This is the person I would

like to be,

this is the person I would

like you to think
of me as . . .

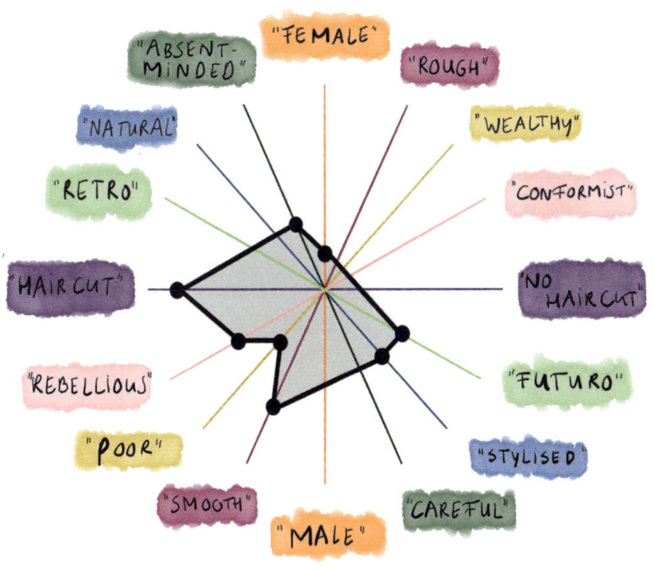

. . . this person who sits on these various spectrums in these various positions.'

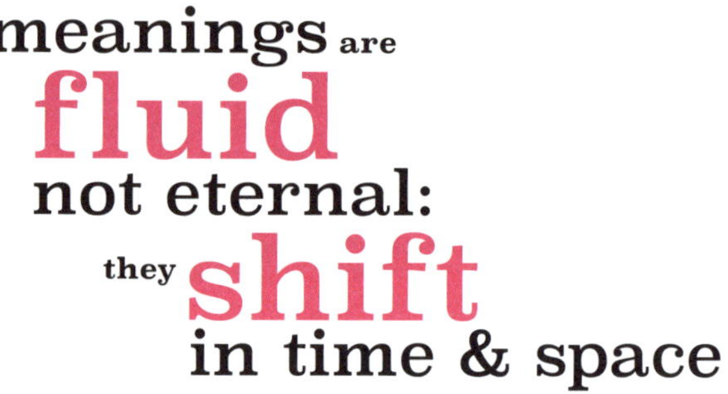

Axes come and go and change value. They are always in motion.

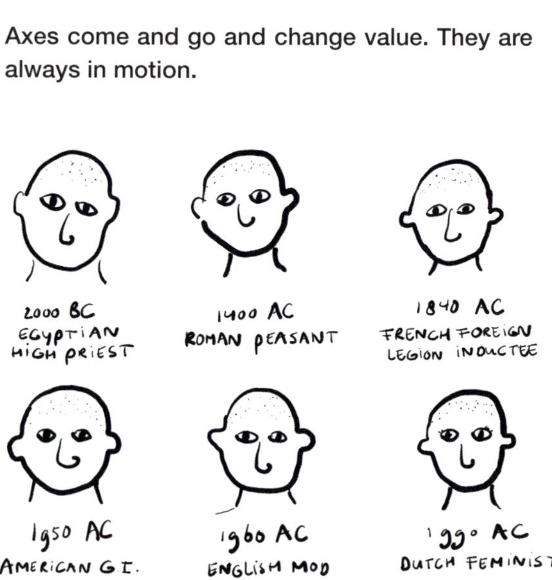

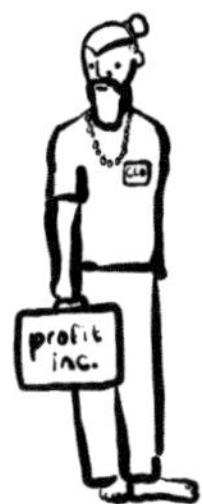

In the 1960s, the axis 'short / long' was very highly charged. A British man with long hair was automatically a hippy, part of the counterculture, probably effeminate and almost certainly anti-war. That has since changed: executives in tech companies have long hair; as do pro-gun militia members.

Occasionally an axis will go out of fashion – think of powdered wigs . . . nobody is particularly interested in those any more. And then new ones come into being, such as the 'fade / no-fade' axis (in buzzcuts), or the 'mono-coloured / multicoloured' axis.

The practice of braiding hair, which has been around for millennia, has countless lineages all over the world, and new distinctions come into being each day.

So if you look at haircuts you can see a whole new stylistic language evolving, and some of the terms in the language keep changing value. How the haircut reads depends on when and where it is being read, and by whom.

The same goes for any piece of art.

Sometimes these readings can get very
complex

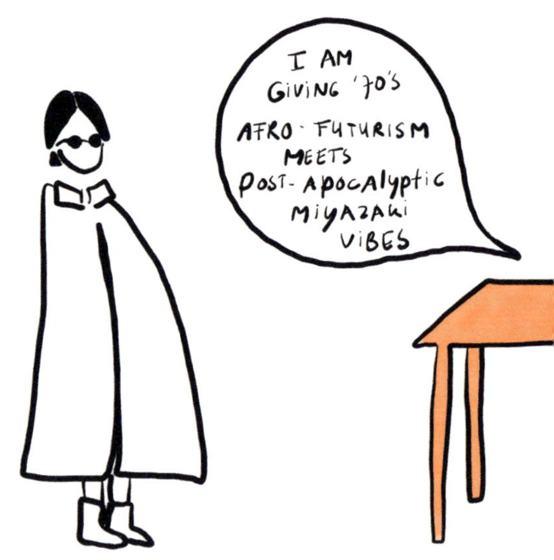

And sometimes they are simple.

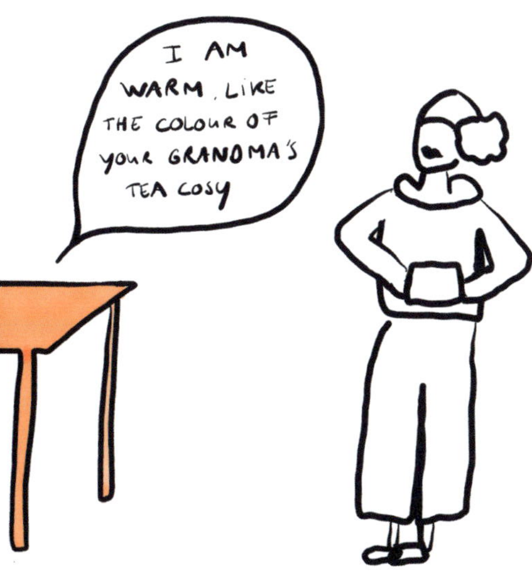

A piece of art doesn't have to be a piece of art for everybody. It does not have to cause feelings in everyone.

Art doesn't have to be eternal. There could be something that works as art for a few people for a few weeks, for a lot of people for a hundred years, for one person for a lifetime, for a small number of people for a thousand years. There are all sorts of levels.

It is always a conversation, even if there is only one person involved in the conversation. You might make art as a conversation with yourself.

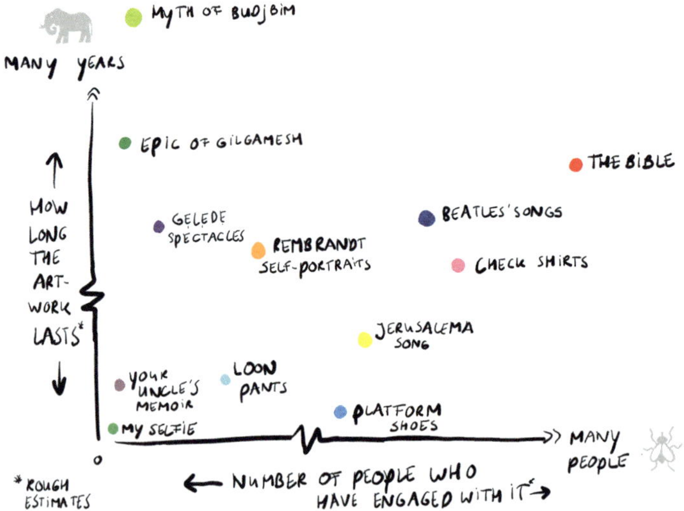

There's local art, topical art, tourist art, and there's art that seems to exist longer than that, or seems to spread further.

A meme that goes out on social media may reach a lot of people, and do all the things that another piece of art does – but perhaps not for very long. In two weeks' time there might be other things to look at and nobody is interested in that meme any longer.

That doesn't mean it wasn't important. It just means it was a short-lived piece of art. It did not have a long life, like some insects don't have a long life.

And then there are other pieces, for instance the Gẹlẹdẹ spectacles of the Yoruba in Nigeria, which have never had a worldwide audience, but have existed a very long time. And there are things that have had a huge audience and have existed a very long time, like the Pyramids.

Think of an ecosystem with a huge variety of members. Just as it is undecidable whether butterflies are more important than elephants, it's undecidable whether pop songs are more important than symphonies.

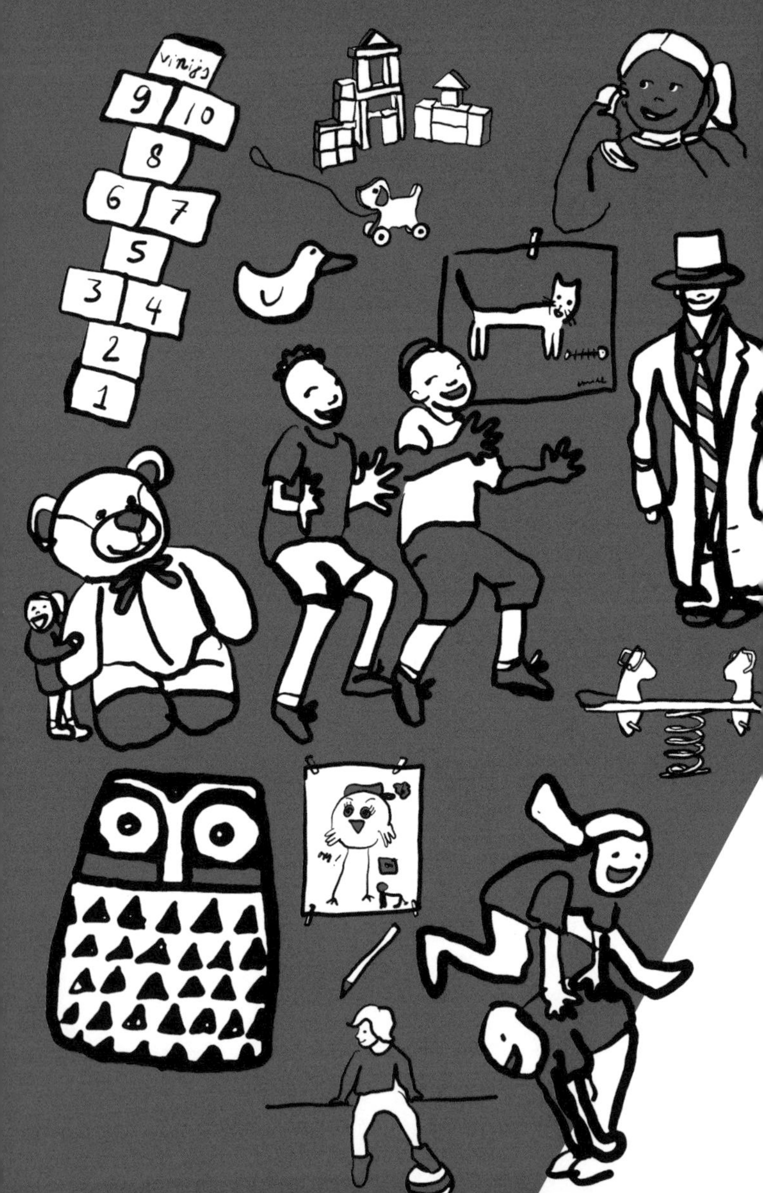

vinijs
9 10
8
6 7
5
3 4
2
1

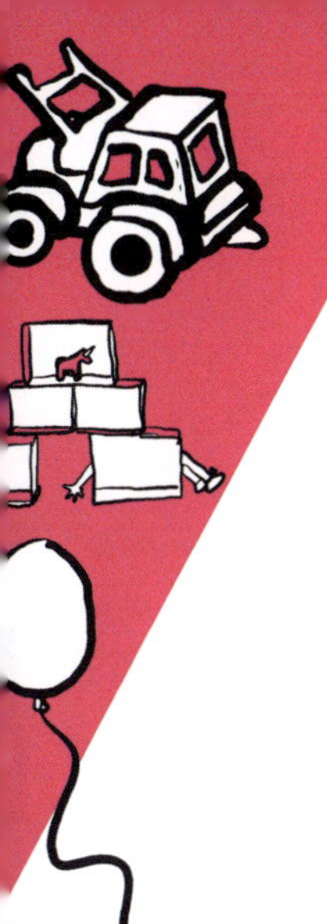

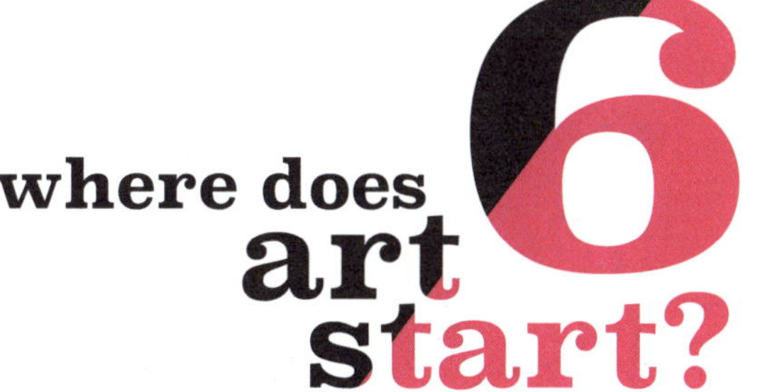

where does art start? 6

To understand why art
is an important human activity,

let's look at

play

and how
that works for children.

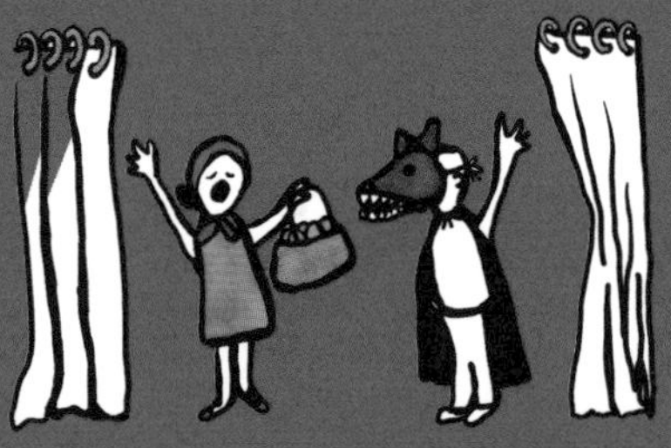

People used to think of play as frivolous time, the way many people now think about art. We all understand now that children learn through play. Children are learning machines. In the first few years of their lives they absorb vast amounts of information about how words fit together, what you can say to your mother that you wouldn't say to a stranger; about what things you can eat and what you can't; about how to share the playground with others; about how to buy things in a shop . . . it's a huge amount of stuff, and a lot of it is learnt in the spirit of playing.

Watch a group of children playing. On the one hand we have Celeste and Theresa sitting in a corner pouring water back and forth from a jug into a cup. Nearby, Melanie, Zolani and Blaine are pretending to make dinner with some pots and pans, adding imaginary ingredients. Shiv, Tim, Nuala and Nick are competing with each other over in the other corner – seeing who can jump highest. John is going down the slide over and over again. Mathilde is talking to her doll, telling her a story.

The play of the children spans a spectrum. At the one end you could say they are finding out about how the materials of the real world work – how water works, how their bodies work, how strong or flexible or sharp things are. At the other end of the spectrum there is 'Let's pretend' – the invention of games or scenarios, of other worlds that don't really exist.

Children move fluidly between these two states of mind and often combine them. In the varieties of children's play we see the origins of not only art and science but many other adult behaviours, like caring and nurturing and philosophising and deceiving.

All young animals
want to play
and
humans
more than most

Children don't have to be encouraged to play. They love doing it. We see them jumping and running and competing and developing their bodies, taking things apart and broadening their knowledge of the world.

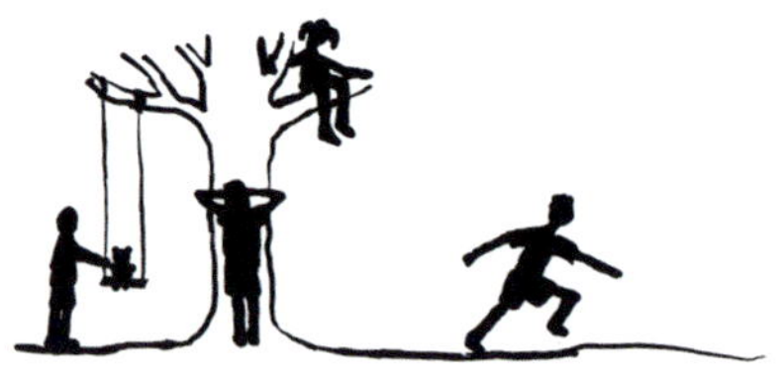

The pleasure of play evolved to keep us playing!

The benefits of play make obvious evolutionary sense when we're talking about play that explores physical development, such as coordination and muscle control.

What 'muscles' are children developing when they play 'Let's pretend'?

The most obvious one is the 'imagination' muscle. Imagining is the great human skill.

It's how we project our minds into possible futures; where we create and test projects that do not presently exist.

We do this by practising it in play.

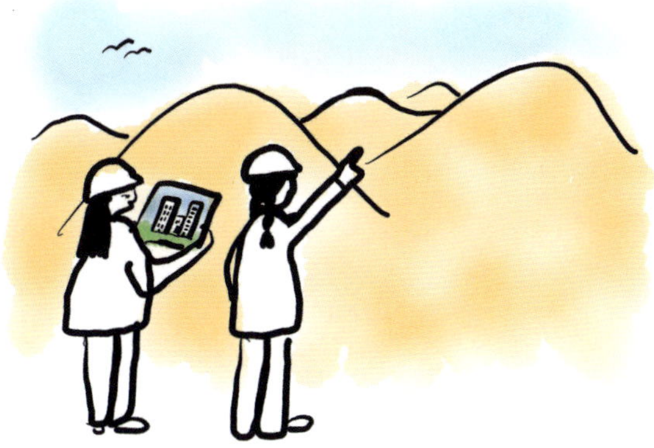

Children imagine other possible worlds in which they are, for instance, parents, doctors, soldiers, babies, princesses, monsters . . . and they explore these worlds by paying attention to their feelings about them. If you play Mummy and Baby, for example, or Doctor and Patient, or Police and Thief, what you are doing is modelling sets of relationships and enjoying your feelings about them.

Play is where we start to discover how we feel about things. Feelings are the reward for playing. Play is how children learn.

Playing with possible choices in a safe (imaginary, or fictional) environment and trying out the individual and communal feelings that come with these choices develops us as individuals and as social beings.

So what does this have to do with art?

Here's a proposal: art is how adults play.

Art is the continuation of play into adulthood. We keep playing as adults because we need to keep learning. Play is research.

In art we research our feelings. Artists are feelings merchants – a piece of art is something designed to trigger feelings. Our feelings guide us as we move into new futures, either by tempting us on, or frightening us away.

PLAY IS HOW CHILDREN LEARN
ART IS HOW ADULTS PLAY

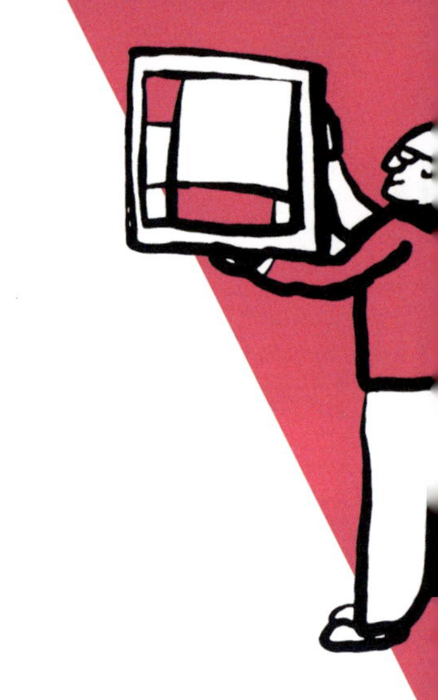

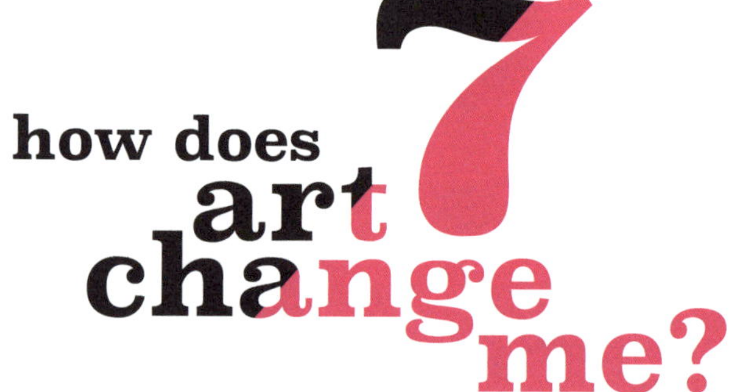
how does **art** change me?

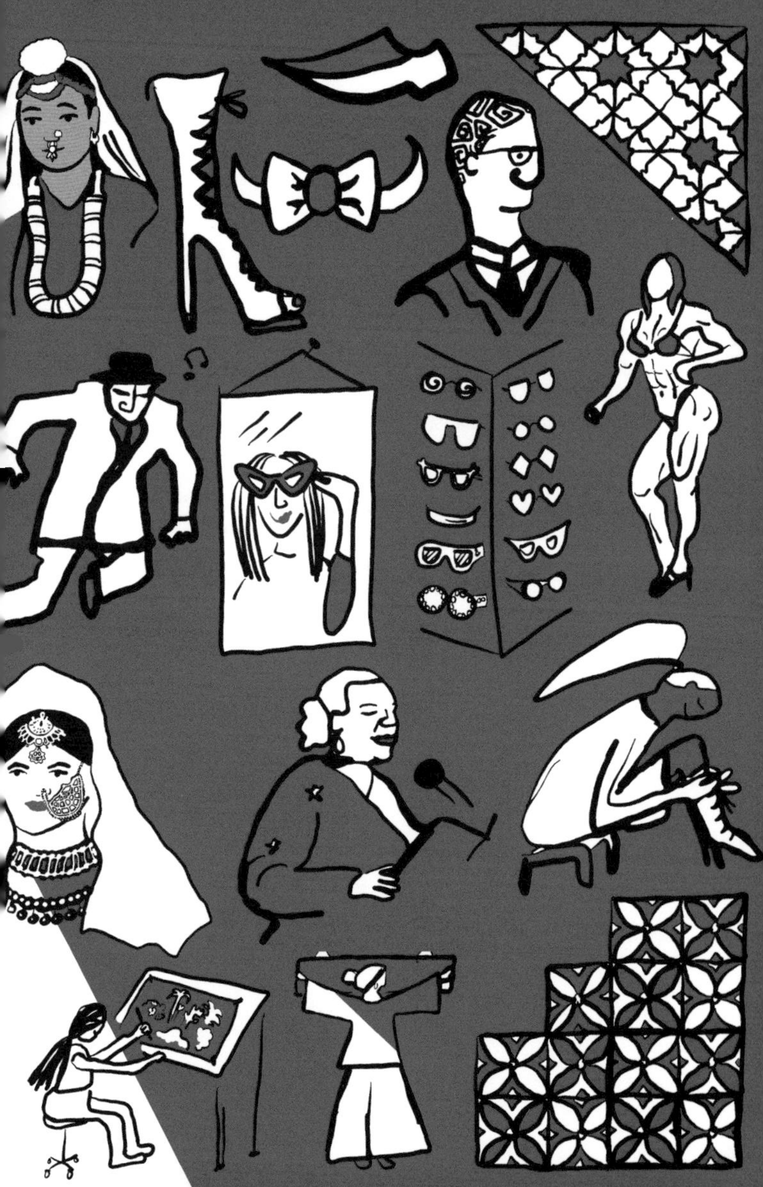

What is it that I really like?

The musician Jon Hassell
used to say that this is
the most important question
you can ask yourself.

You recall those moments in life when you've seen or heard something that has stopped you in your tracks. The feeling of being overpowered, entranced by something, of wanting to see it more and more or to hear it again and again: that's when you know you really like something.

That moment of discovery lights a flame inside you.

We're used to the idea that we avoid the things that hurt us – hot things, sharp things, stressful things – but we're less used to the idea that we can navigate our way through life by following the things that truly and deeply please us.

Paying attention to the things we love and that make us feel good and happy isn't an indulgence, but a sensible use of our faculties. That's why we evolved them. The problem is that those faculties are constantly overwhelmed by things that other people wished that we liked.

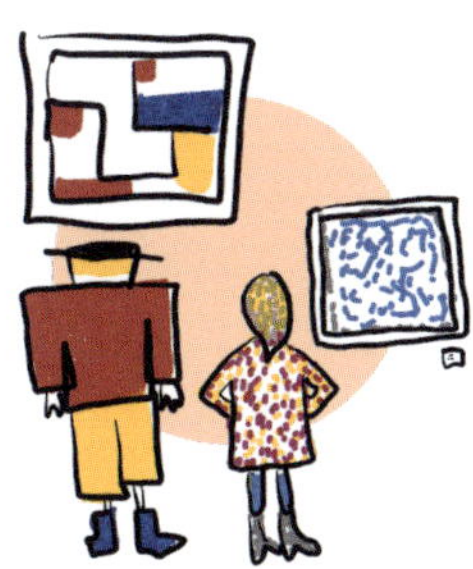

To discover what you really like is to have a guiding star and to be able to navigate through the blizzard of all the voices telling you what you ought to like – the advertisers, politicians, influencers, ideologues, algorithms. It is your claim to independence of mind (even if a billion other people like it too!).

A crucial part of self-realisation is being able to distinguish between our shallow likes and deep likes. Shallow likes are the fleeting ones, the induced desires that advertising and its tentacles in social media create in us. Deep likes are based in who we are, in our most personal preferences and values. They are persistent and generate feelings of happiness.

Through art, you can investigate the kind of feelings you want to have, and where to get them. Art gives us the chance to answer the question: what is it that I really like?

This investigation into our likes can be done through artworks as elaborate as a novel, as vague as an abstract painting, as direct as punk and as subtle as a slightly tighter pony tail.

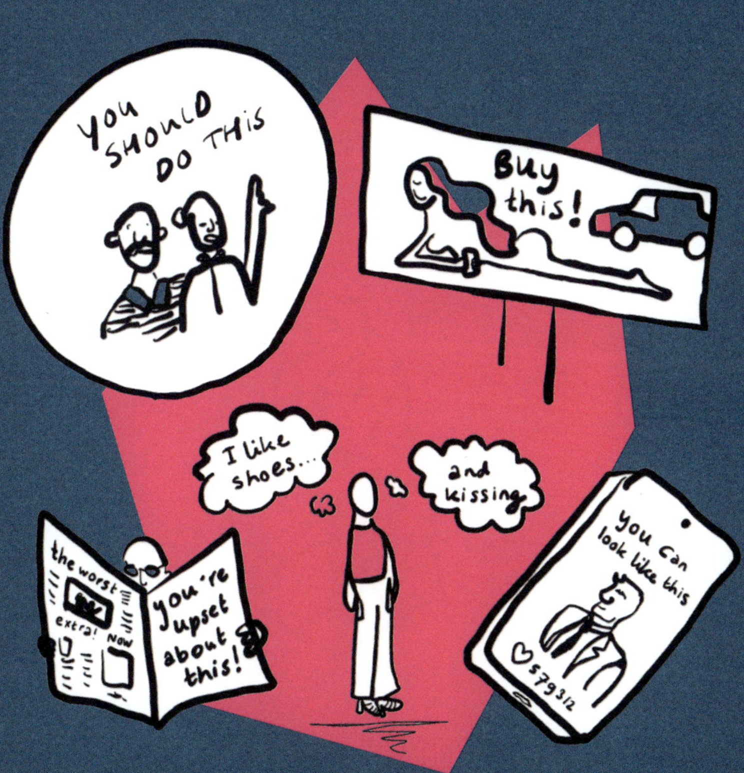

you SHOULD DO THIS
BUY this!
I like shoes...
and kissing
the worst
extra!
NOW
you're upset about this!
you can look like this
579312

art changes
how we
feel about our
feelings

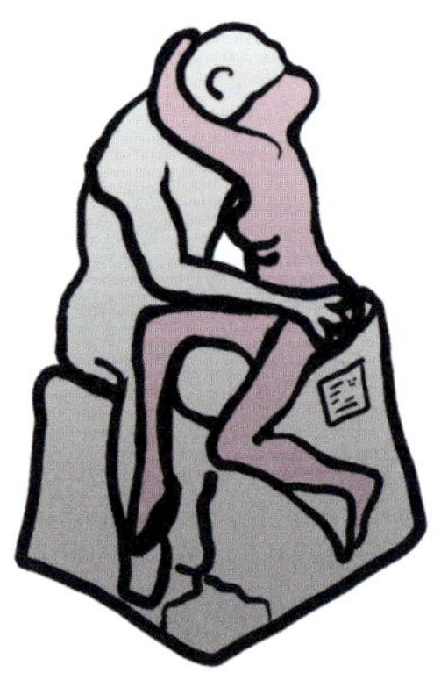

How we notice them, how we respond to them, how we compare them, how we make use of them.

People might react to an artwork
in many different ways:

'Somebody else has the same feeling as I do.'

or

'I remember this feeling.'

or

'This is a way I can identify and locate this feeling.'

or

'This is a place in which I can indulge in this feeling.'

or

'This is a new feeling about something old.'

or

'I find this feeling a relief.'

or

'This feeling makes me aware of something that
is missing from my life.'

or

'I now have feelings about something that never
provoked any feelings in me before.'

or

'This feeling makes me feel . . .' (apply any adjective)

What an artist chooses to write or make drawings or songs about, can draw our attention to certain worlds. It tells us that somebody takes something seriously, perhaps finds it beautiful or threatening, and invites us to rethink how we feel about it.

The things we care about are the things we make art about. We frame them with our attention.

Art is proof of care.

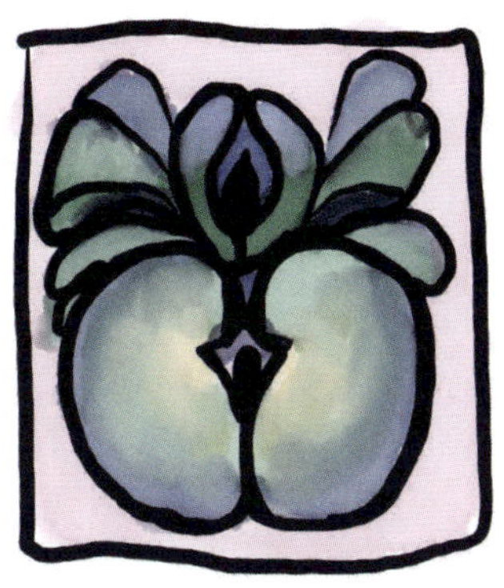

'human beings
don't see what is
in front
of them

they see what is
important
to them'

CARMODY GREY, theologian

Sometimes art is showing us what is wrong or good or fun about the world we inhabit, but other times it's showing us a made-up world, with, for instance, trolls and mermaids, or magical old-lady detectives. What does it mean to find out you like something that is out of this world?

Certain forms of art get criticised for being escapist. There's an assumption that good art must always be difficult in some way.

But what's wrong with escaping? What's wrong with wanting to experience another reality that is better than this one? What does that tell you about this one? If you find out what 'better' means for you, you have a richer understanding of the world you're in and what it is missing.

If you find, for example, that you're drawn to listening to types of music where not much happens, where there are big open spaces, it may make you realise that you want to live in a world where there's less stimulus . . . That's important to know! Wanting less stimulus can be quite a radical message in a world where you are exposed to ten thousand adverts a day.

Art can form a contrast to the world you're in, and you find yourself thinking: 'What is it about this other world that I like, that isn't in my world?'

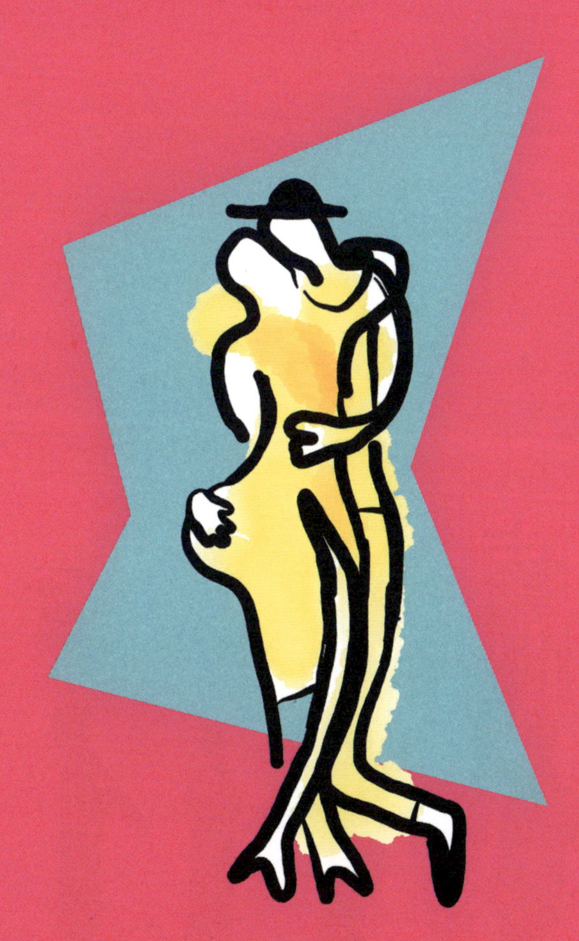

For the writer bell hooks, art exists to consider what is possible – how else things could be – not just what is.

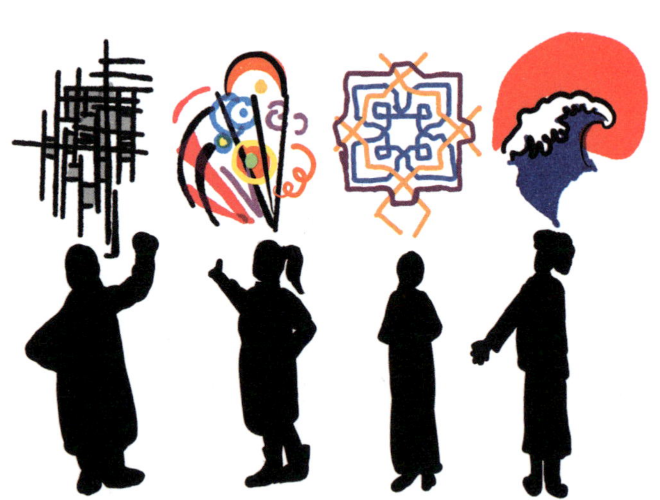

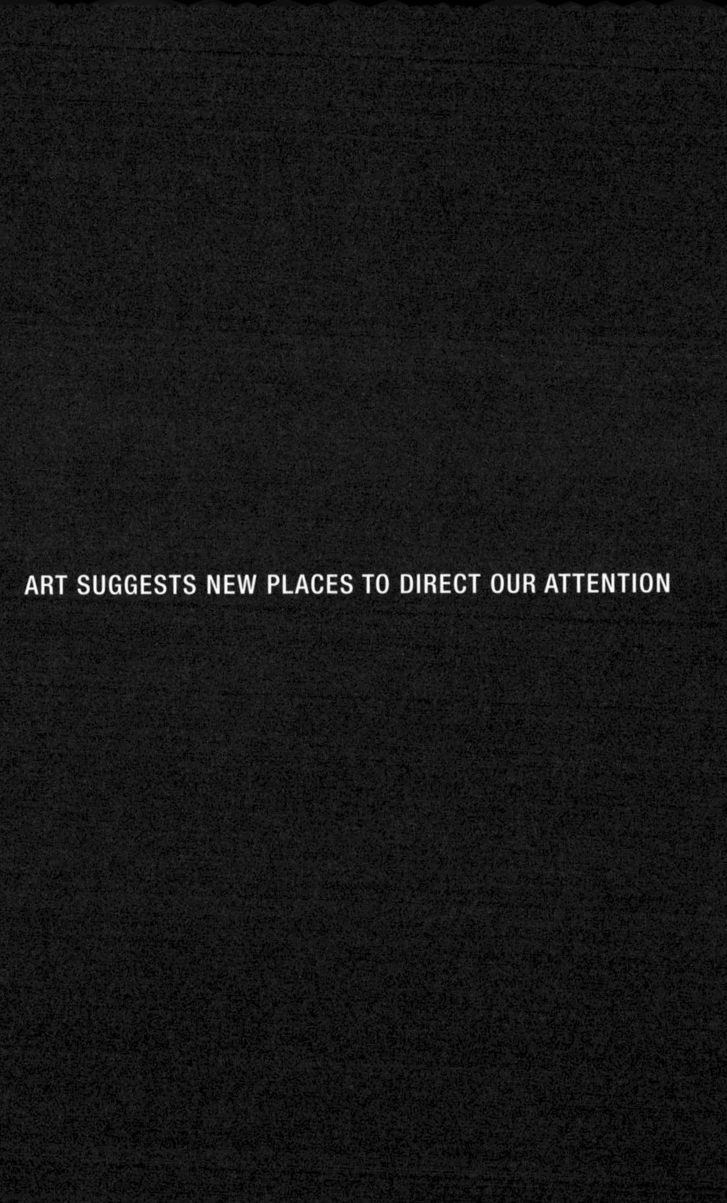
ART SUGGESTS NEW PLACES TO DIRECT OUR ATTENTION

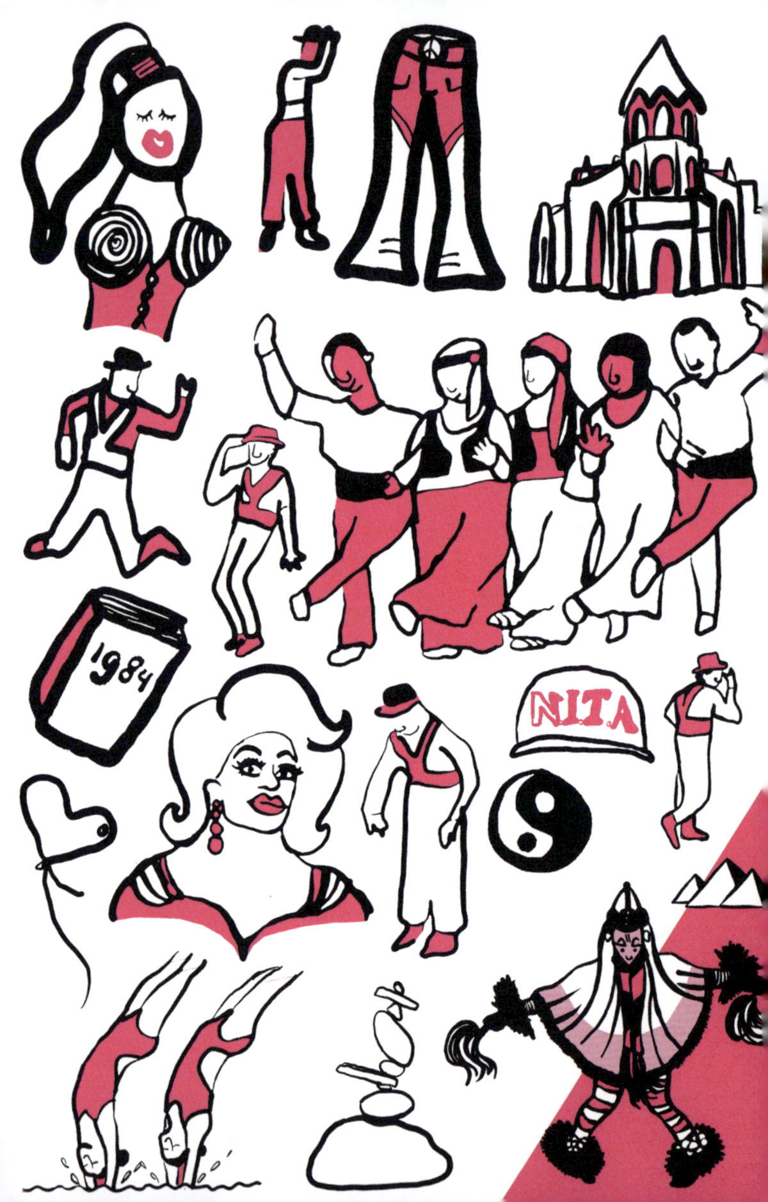
1984
NITA

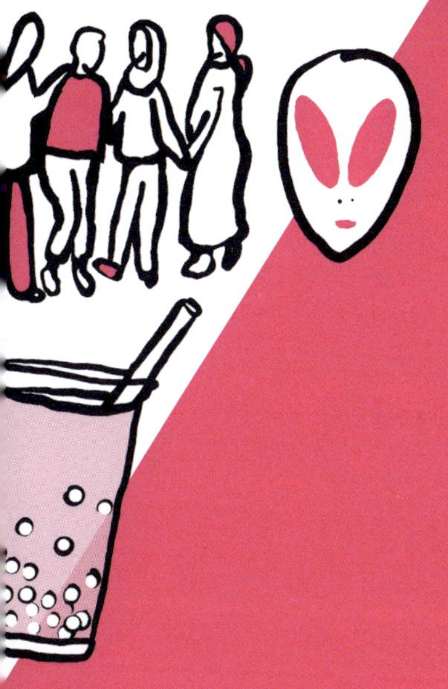

how does
art
change
8
us?

art
is where we
share
dreams

(and nightmares)

There are 8 billion people in the world, and they're more different from each other than humans have ever been before. Turn the clock back a million years and all humans in a given landscape are engaged in pretty similar activities, just like all elephants in the same landscape are engaged in pretty similar activities now. There would have been local differences – in habits, style, customs – but most activities of life would have been recognisable.

There are people doing jobs that most of us do not understand at all, making items whose function is a complete mystery to the average person (say a birefringent tuner or some forehearth channel blocks). In fact, most of the things we use during a normal day – a computer, the bus, a phone, the plumbing, the radio – are actually a mystery to us. We might know vaguely how they work but we wouldn't know how to fix a single one of them. But we don't need to! – because somebody else does. We are the beneficiaries of thousands of brains, not just the one we carry inside our skull.

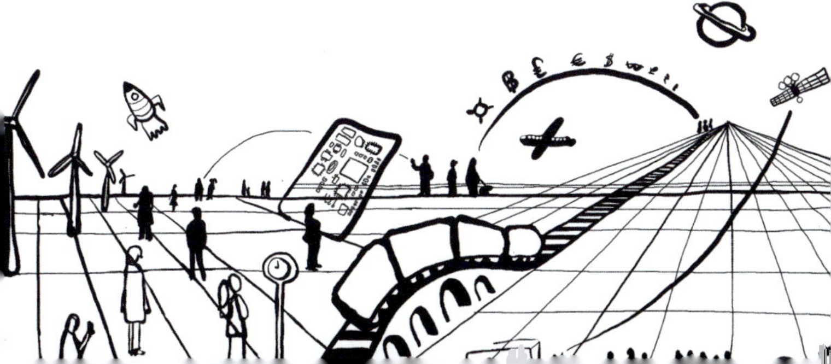

As an example, imagine how many people are involved in getting you to work . . . Let's start with the bus to the local station from where you'll take the train.

Who invented the bus?
Who made all the parts of the bus?
Who taught them how to do this?
Who tested the bus for safety?
Who drove the bus to the station?
Who taught this driver how to drive?
Who designed the bus driver test?
Who wrote the questions?
Who scored them?
Who came up with the road signs and the traffic lights?
Who installed those?
Who transported them to their locations?
Who wrote the transport laws and regulations?
Who made the machine that reads your transport card?
Who made the parts for that machine?
Who designed them?
Who wrote the books this designer studied from?
Who gave the designer access to them?
Who maintains the library administration system?
Who stores the library data?
Who got the petrol for the bus into the country?
Who invented 'refining' oil?
Who runs the oilfields?
Who runs the shipping networks?
Who runs the money exchange facilities?
Who translates between the countries involved?
Who pays that person?
Who designed the chip in your transport card?
Who gathered the materials needed?
Who checked on their safety?
Who transported the materials?
Who negotiated the price for the materials?

We're not even at the station yet and you've used the products of the brains of literally tens of thousands of people. You don't have to carry so much in your own brain.

What happened is that we went from being generalists – people who could forage, hunt, cook, make shelters, fight, and store all the knowledge necessary for those activities individually – to people who could survive by doing pretty much just one thing: specialists.

We can store information externally, with other members of our communities, countries and groups. But that brings a new danger.

How do all these wildly different brains stay connected? What can hold us together so that the whole system still has some integrity, some sense of unity? So that we can do all those complicated things together?

Art is one of the things that binds people together. Or on the other hand, allows them to define themselves as separate. It's a way of saying: 'I belong with this body of ideas and feelings, not that body of ideas and feelings.' That is what fashion, interior design and popular culture are often about. What's the difference between a Bauhaus house and a Laura Ashley house – what does each choice say?

one says

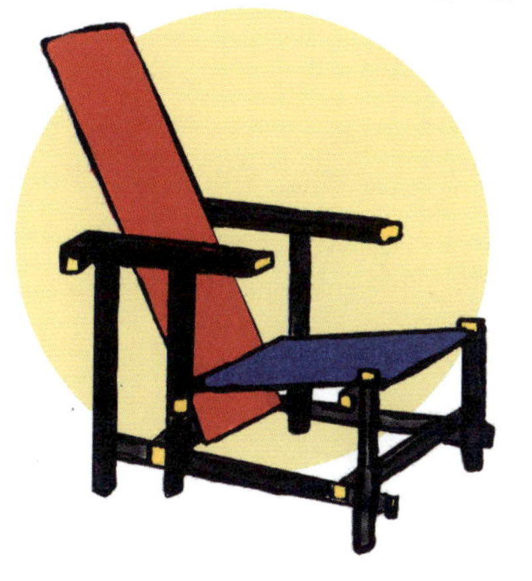

'I think ornament is superfluous. I like things made by industrial processes that don't hide their origin or try to be something else. A chair is a chair so let's enjoy it for what it is.'

the other says

'I want to surround myself with pretty, natural things.'

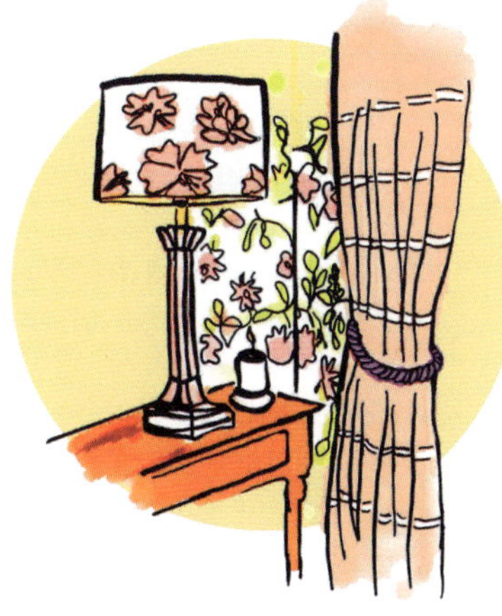

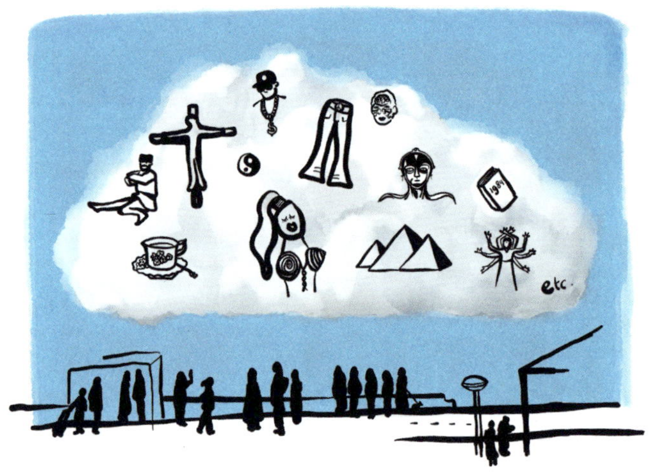

This cultural conversation – the sum total of all our opinions about what is cool and what isn't, what is nice and what isn't – this is 'the cloud': the one that really matters to us.

Art is that cloud; a reservoir of shared experiences that gives us ways of sharing complex feelings and ideas with each other. It's the lifeblood, the lubricant, the circulatory system of community. The maintenance of community.

Civilisation is shared imagination.

We often use cultural artefacts (like the Rolling Stones or Monty Python, Yoko Ono, the Riordan family, Spock, Audre Lorde, Kafka, Conchita Wurst, Fela Kuti, Beyoncé, Aki Kaurismäki) as identifiers of certain hard-to-describe feeling-ideas that we want to refer to.

Those 'feeling-ideas' might be things like:

feeling constrained by the conservatism of your post-war parents, or

making fun of over-narrow, reductive thinking,

wanting to imagine a world that doesn't have simple good/bad distinctions,

believing the human spirit is stronger than any oppressive government,

aligning with a non-binary approach to gender,

being critical of bureaucratic procedures,

preferring a more rational mode of being.

How do communities change their minds in the absence of clear statements on moral, legal and philosophical positions that we can all take a vote on? How does it happen that societies shift their opinions?

An example of such a shift is how not adhering to a traditional gender identity is becoming more acceptable in the Western world. That probably isn't because of legislation, but because more people somehow or other became comfortable with the idea of a gender spectrum (rather than just 'male' and 'female'), and with the further idea that any point on that spectrum is a place you can live.

One of the primary ways we become comfortable with that sort of societal shift is by first of all modelling it, or seeing it being modelled, in art.

(remember: art is safe)

Many musicians of the sixties made it acceptable for men to embrace feelings previously regarded as 'un-masculine' and also for women to embrace feelings previously regarded as 'unfeminine'.

This didn't need to be widely articulated to be felt. Instead people saw it and found it aesthetically attractive. They felt it was right and exciting for them.

Feelings, especially socially shared ones, guide us towards a sense of what we think is right, but they also guide us away from things. People pay a lot of attention to what other people are thinking, and they start to feel the friction of being not fully in agreement with others. This can arouse feelings of anxiety or triumph . . . but it doesn't pass unnoticed.

We are acutely aware of difference. Of our positioning in the scheme of things. Art helps us identify the sources of those feelings and anxieties, gives us a way of locating them and sharing them.

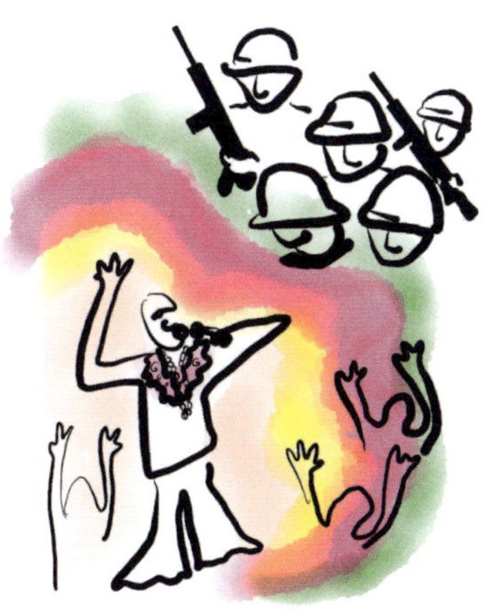

Soap operas, for example, are good places for this kind of social conversation. They provide a safe, neutral space through which sensitive topics can be broached and discussed. And they are pretty much universal. They often become important centers of national and even international conversations.

In Hangzhou factory workers bring each other up to date with episodes of the soaps they missed due to revolving shift patterns. In Trinidad, a few neighbours might show up when the soap starts. In Egypt, some families sit down together after the Iftar meal to watch the Ramadan soap operas. A Rwandan soap opera that aimed to improve inter-ethnic relationships was found most successful when the audience listened to it in a social setting: they discussed what happened afterwards and later reported more positive inter-ethnic attitudes.

It's a way for people to take the local cultural temp-erature. By discussing the developments in their favourite soap opera they're adjusting themselves to the new realities in their societies, and they are thinking about it from the position of all the characters involved in the soap opera. They are jointly involved in thinking something through, about which they can develop their own feelings, because it's fictional.

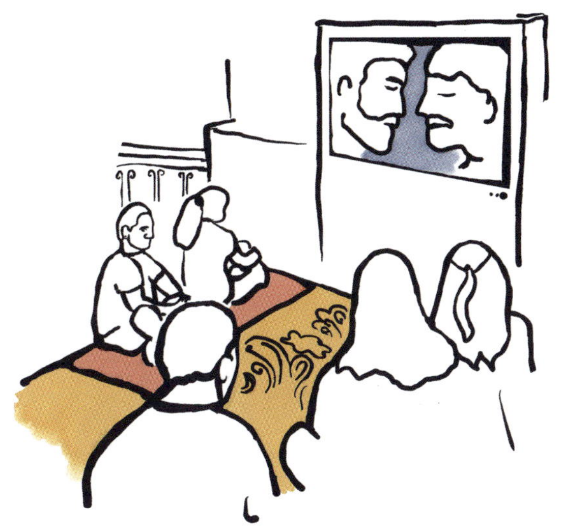

Why does it matter that it is fictional?

because:

1. they can know about the feelings of all involved (because they 'know' the characters involved), and

2. there are no real-world consequences to their thoughts.

being **together in art** is an **agreement** to share some **feelings** with each other

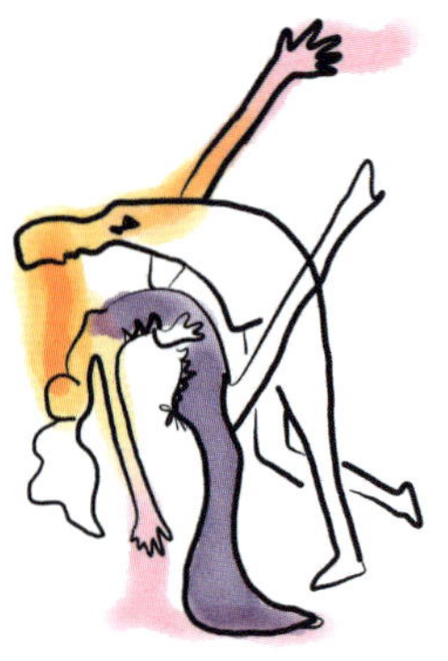

That involves being vulnerable together, opening up to each other.

Art can be a way that people who might be wildly different in many aspects can share something.
At the level of feelings we can be equals.
We all have them.

Especially in the consumer era, we've been encouraged to think of ourselves as separate and independent individuals, whereas our strength as a species comes from our ability to continually adjust and cooperate. Art is one of the most powerful ways of doing that, of finding out where our common grounds and our differences lie.

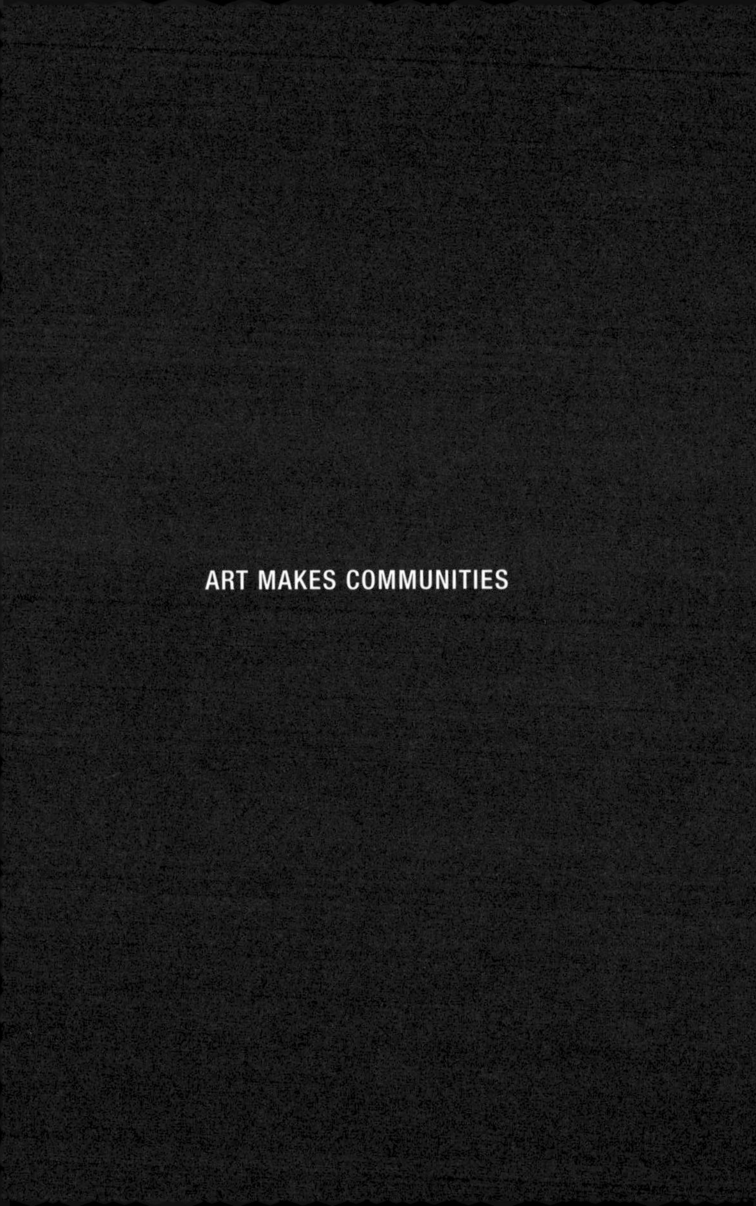
ART MAKES COMMUNITIES

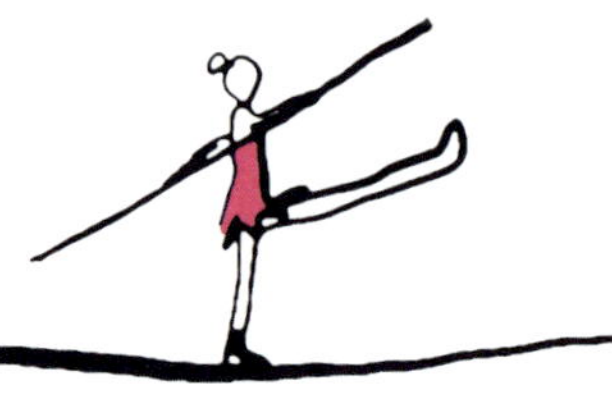

Central to the idea of a cultural conversation is the notion of surrender. Surrender is what we do when we stop trying to control things, when we let something happen to us.

All humans voluntarily engage in activities that involve surrender – sex, drugs, religion, art – and very often these are considered peak experiences. In each of those we deliberately put ourselves into a situation whose reward is to be carried along by something 'bigger than us'.

Surrender becomes an active verb. It's a way of stepping back from individualism, stop being 'me' for a little while and enjoying being 'us'. This voluntary suspension of control allows us to have experiences and feelings that are new to us, that didn't originate in our conscious brains. Isn't this what we also call learning?

As a species, we're so phenomenally good at control, that we tend to think it must be the right posture for every problem.

But genuinely novel situations don't come with ready-made control strategies: we have to under-stand them by letting them happen to us. If that's too dangerous, we can simulate them, and let the simulations happen to us.

That's what we're doing in art.

If we don't learn to make a balance between control and surrender, if we only know how to control, we end up in a world shrunken to the bits that we can still control. The raw wild world develops and leaves us behind, playing Solitaire on our phones.

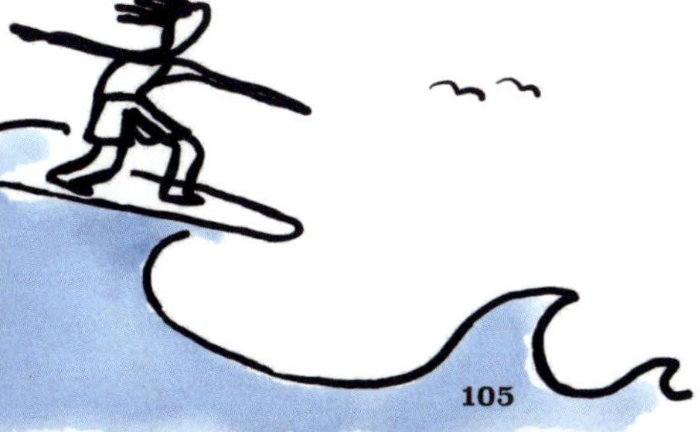

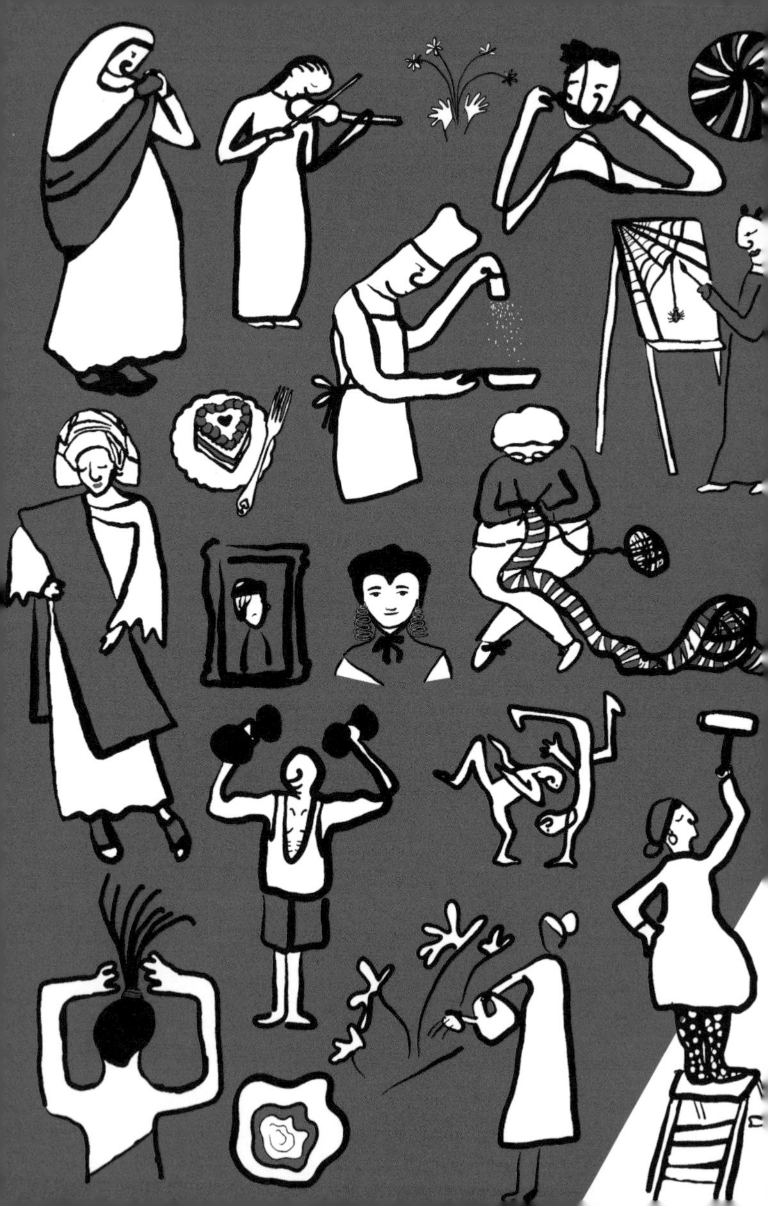

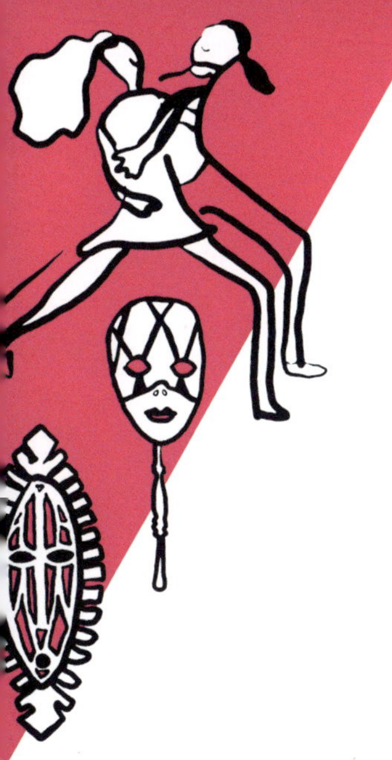

we
start
worlds

9

In art, we try out new possible worlds and other ways of being, by paying attention to our feelings about them. Art allows us to share complicated concepts and feelings with each other. This cultural conversation opens doors to shifts – in ourselves and in society.

Art shepherds change.

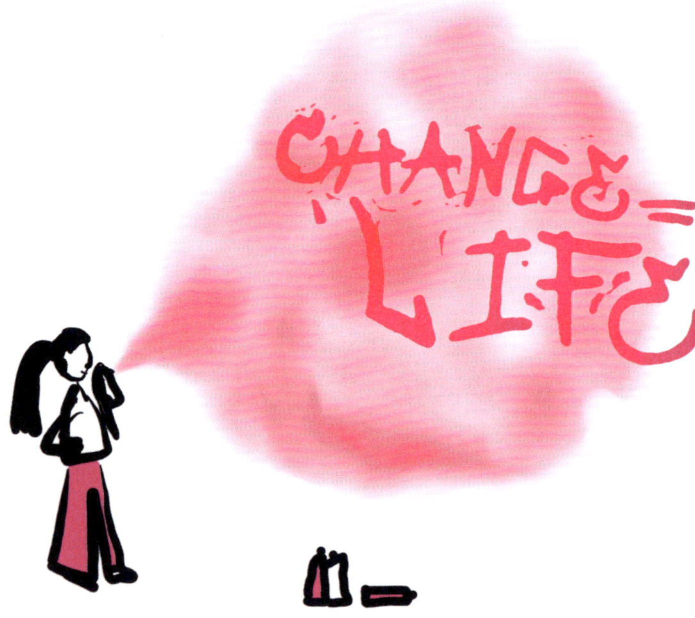

When we think of shaping the future, we can start with ideas about ideal worlds. Utopianism is imagining we could come up with the final definitive idea of how the world should be, and then sit back and enjoy it. But we will never succeed in that project: there will always be work to do because nothing stays the same for long.

Writer Stewart Brand says of buildings:

'You don't finish a building: you start it …'

. . . and that is the way we could think about artworks and, probably, our lives. As artists, we don't finish it: we start it. It goes on to have a life without us, a life we didn't predict.

Let's start admiring gardeners as much as we admire architects. It will always be unfinished.

Individuals articulate ideas but it's communities that produce, support and nurture them. A single flower is the product of a whole landscape. Just as there is no such thing as a self-made flower, there's no such thing as a self-made human.

This vision says that culture is alive and different every time we look at it. This is why curators have become such important figures: they are testing and exercising this process, seeing how things fit together now and what their current cultural valency is. This approach thinks of artworks as 'alive', not 'finished'.

Most importantly, perhaps, we might start to think the same way about ourselves: that we are unfinished (and unfinishable) beings whose task is constantly to re-examine and remix our ideas and our identities.

An attitude like this equips us better to deal with planetary emergencies like climate change and the crises of governance. For although we will certainly need new regulations, laws and technical advances, beyond all of those we will need imagination, new imaginings.

We need to be able to visualise the sensations of our possible futures to imagine how we can live and thrive and feel competent in the new realities we face. And we will need new models of human interaction that teach us how to cooperate better.

The climate crisis, the wars, the increasing inequality – the world urgently needs new ways of understanding where we are and where we could go. Art is one of the ways we can do this, helping us feel new futures and understanding the powers of community to bring about the changes we need. Science makes models of things so we can understand how they work. Art makes models of things so we can understand how we work.

Politics all too often makes the individual feel left outside, without agency or power. We will only succeed when we empower people – all sorts of people, not just the experts and professionals – all over the world to have the confidence to imagine new futures. Just as we need science to tell us how the changing world is, we need art to help find out how we feel about it. We need those feelings to guide our decisions and values. Science discovers, art digests.

If we reimagine the human project as being about means rather than ends – about making a mindset and a sense of sensible procedures rather than designing an Ultimate Heaven-on-Earth – we will get better results.

We need new means, not old ends.

poems,
songs,
novels,
furniture design,
gemstone collections,
architecture,
sock puppets,
exhibitions,
facial expressions,
picture frames,
graffiti,
installations,
creative coding,

operas,
nicknames,
headscarves,
face painting,
fantasies,
slogans,
signature dance moves,
tattoos,
manifestos,
love songs,
protest posters,
typography,
zines,

let's begin new

shrines,
melodies,
bathroom tiles,
glitter,
eyeshadow,
cat pictures,
memes,
video games,
textile design,
documentaries,
plays,
wedding vows,
rhymes,
easter eggs,
puzzles,
street parties,
flower arrangements,
clowning,
crocheting,

festivals,
cosplay,
moustaches,
earrings,
cakes,
funny walks,
love letters,
self-portraits,
watercolours,
frosting,
needlepoint,
kinetic sculptures,
movies,
rolling ball machines,
land art,
trapeze acts,
wigs,
illustrations,

spoken word,
scrapbooks,
chanting,
labyrinths,
wood carvings,
origami,
Sunday suits,
nose rings,
hijabs,
mime,
pottery,
water ornaments,
selfies,
statues,
flip-flops,

hoodies,
daydreams,
haiku,
glasses,
monuments,
TV shows,
podcasts,
sidewalk chalk,
funfairs,
memoirs,
rituals,
altars,
cartoons,
nursery rhymes,
games,
herbaria,
galleries,
playgrounds,

worlds

that we like

through our

notebooks,
journals,
handshakes,
psalms,
bandanas,
lighting,
curtains,
waltzing,
drums,
papier-mâché,
paperweights,
doilies,
printmaking,
murals,
web design,
radio shows,
emblems,

screensavers,
museums,
gardens,
specialty coffees,
sunshades,
lipsticks,
mum jeans,
dad jokes,
silverware,
sewing patterns,
audiobooks,
buzzwords,
captions,
trends,
ice-cream flavours,
comedy specials,
whistling . . .

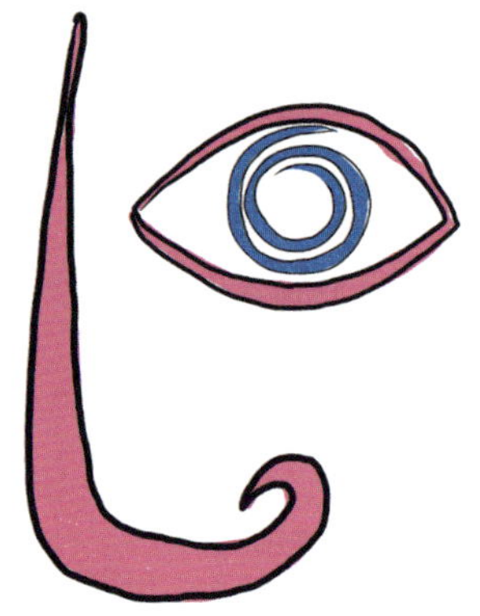

If we want a new world, we have to start
making it right now . . .

. . . actually we are making it right now in
every decision we take.

To acknowledge that is the first step to
doing it consciously. If we want a world
where women are listened to, for example,
we start by listening to women.

In whatever we are doing, we have to make
it as though we are in that new world.
By making objects, systems, experiences
and collaborations that belong to that world,
it comes into being.

Live the world you want.

What kind of world would
that be for you?

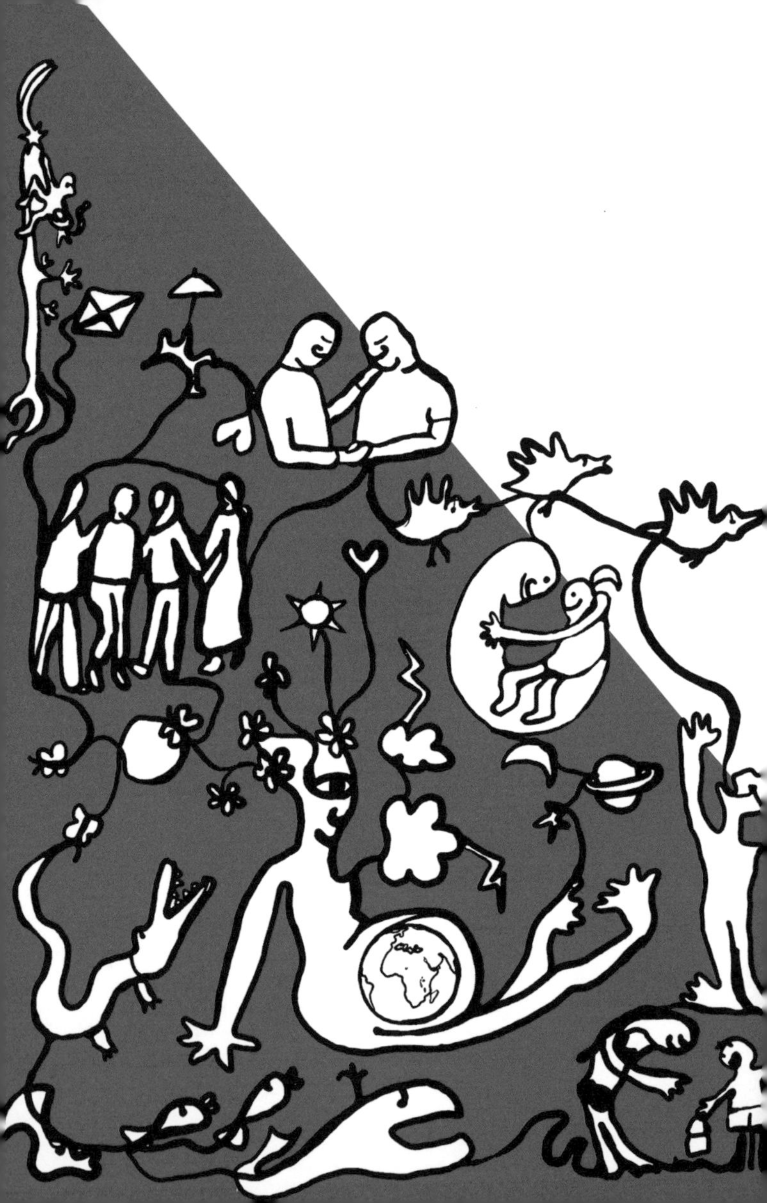

10
wish

A wish for this book would be that it causes us to
reassess the value of these two things:

playing and feeling.

And to realise that what we need is already inside
us, and that art – playing and feeling – is a way of
discovering it.

There's a beautiful sculpture by Giuseppe Penone.
He took a tree trunk and cut away most of the
growth of the tree, leaving behind what had been
there when the tree was ten years old.

Inside big tree is baby tree.
Inside you is little you.
It's always there.

Brian Eno   Bette A.

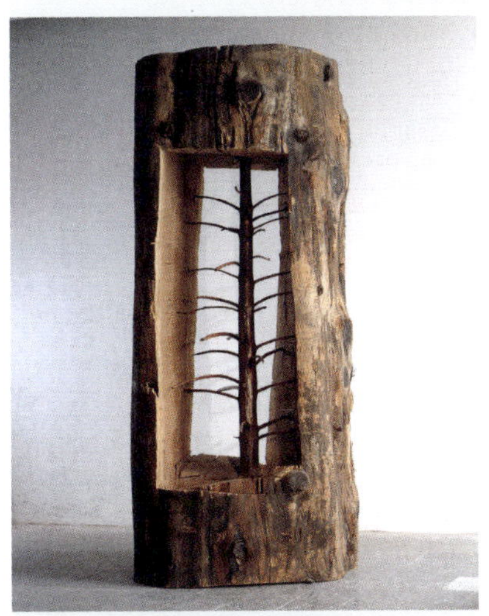

Giuseppe Penone, *Albero porta* (*Door Tree*), 1993
Sequoia wood
photo © Luigi Gariglio

bibliography

Most of these writers wrote more than one great book.
We've just listed one for each.

Alexander, Christopher, et al: A PATTERN LANGUAGE: TOWNS, BUILDINGS, CONSTRUCTION

Alexander, Jon: CITIZENS: WHY THE KEY TO FIXING IS ALL OF US

Angelou, Maya: AND STILL I RISE: A BOOK OF POEMS

Baudrillard, Jean: SIMULACRA AND SIMULATION

Beer, Stafford: BRAIN OF THE FIRM

Blamey, Marjorie: THE ILLUSTRATED FLORA OF BRITAIN AND NORTHERN EUROPE

Boyd, Joe: AND THE ROOTS OF RHYTHM REMAIN: A JOURNEY THROUGH GLOBAL MUSIC

Brand, Stewart: HOW BUILDINGS LEARN: WHAT HAPPENS AFTER THEY'RE BUILT

Braudel, Fernand: THE WHEELS OF COMMERCE: CIVILIZATION AND CAPITALISM 15TH–18TH CENTURY, VOL 2

Cage, John: SILENCE: LECTURES AND WRITINGS

Carter, John: PRINTING AND THE MIND OF MAN

Chang, Ha-Joon: 23 THINGS THEY DON'T TELL YOU ABOUT CAPITALISM

Dawkins, Richard: THE SELFISH GENE

Defence Science and Technology Laboratory: PROFILING AND INFLUENCE ANALYSIS: HOW SOAP OPERAS BRING ABOUT CHANGE

Doctorow, Cory: HOW TO DESTROY SURVEILLANCE CAPITALISM

Dunbar, Robin: GROOMING, GOSSIP AND THE EVOLUTION OF LANGUAGE

Ehrenreich, Barbara: DANCING IN THE STREETS: A HISTORY OF COLLECTIVE JOY

Genovese, Eugene D.: ROLL, JORDAN, ROLL: THE WORLD THE SLAVES MADE

Graeber, David, and Wengrow, David: THE DAWN OF EVERYTHING

Griffiths, Jay: WILD: AN ELEMENTAL JOURNEY

Haffner, Sebastian: DEFYING HITLER: A MEMOIR

Hessel, Katy: 'THERE IS A BULLET IN MY BRAIN': THE SEARING ART OF HOLLYWOOD NUN SISTER MARY CORITA. *GUARDIAN*, 26 AUG. 2024

hooks, bell: OUTLAW CULTURE: RESISTING REPRESENTATIONS

Hrdy, Sarah Blaffer: MOTHER NATURE: MATERNAL INSTINCTS AND HOW THEY SHAPE THE HUMAN SPECIES

Keegan, John: THE FACE OF BATTLE:
A STUDY OF AGINCOURT, WATERLOO AND THE SOMME
Kelly, Kevin: OUT OF CONTROL: THE NEW BIOLOGY OF MACHINES, SOCIAL SYSTEMS
AND THE ECONOMIC WORLD
Kiple, Kenneth F. and Ornelas, Kriemhild Coneè (editors): THE CAMBRIDGE WORLD
HISTORY OF FOOD
Lewis-Williams, David: THE MIND IN THE CAVE:
CONSCIOUSNESS AND THE ORIGINS OF ART
Libin, Laurence (editor): THE GROVE DICTIONARY OF MUSICAL INSTRUMENTS
Lorde, Audre: SISTER, OUTSIDER
MacGregor, Neil: A HISTORY OF THE WORLD IN 100 OBJECTS
Massie, Robert K.: PETER THE GREAT: HIS LIFE AND WORLD
Macy, Joanna and Johnstone, Chris: ACTIVE HOPE: HOW TO FACE THE MESS WE'RE IN
WITHOUT GOING CRAZY
Mazzucato, Mariana: THE VALUE OF EVERYTHING:
MAKING AND TAKING IN THE GLOBAL ECONOMY
McNeill, William H.: KEEPING TOGETHER IN TIME: DANCE AND DRILL IN HUMAN HISTORY
Morozov, Evgeny: TO SAVE EVERYTHING, CLICK HERE: TECHNOLOGY, SOLUTIONISM, AND
THE URGE TO FIX PROBLEMS THAT DON'T EXIST
Nabokov, Vladimir: THE GIFT
Peckham, Morse: MAN'S RAGE FOR CHAOS : BIOLOGY, BEHAVIOR AND THE ARTS
Rorty, Richard: CONTINGENCY, IRONY, AND SOLIDARITY
Runciman, David: THE CONFIDENCE TRAP: A HISTORY OF DEMOCRACY IN CRISIS FROM
WORLD WAR I TO THE PRESENT
Rushkoff, Douglas: TEAM HUMAN
Scheidel, Walter: THE GREAT LEVELER: VIOLENCE AND THE HISTORY OF INEQUALITY
FROM THE STONE AGE TO THE TWENTY-FIRST CENTURY
Scott, James C.: SEEING LIKE A STATE: HOW CERTAIN SCHEMES TO IMPROVE THE
HUMAN CONDITION HAVE FAILED
Solms, Mark: THE HIDDEN SPRING: A JOURNEY TO THE SOURCE OF CONSCIOUSNESS
Temelkuran, Ece: HOW TO LOSE A COUNTRY: THE 7 STEPS FROM DEMOCRACY
TO DICTATORSHIP
Turin, Luca, and Sanchez, Tania: PERFUMES: THE GUIDE
Varoufakis, Yanis: TECHNOFEUDALISM: WHAT KILLED CAPITALISM
WIKIPEDIA

acknowledgments and references:
www.whatartdoes.org

• NOTES •

• NOTES •